False Holiness

EXPOSED

False Holiness

EXPOSED

Dr. Bob Hellmann

Take note that the name satan and related names are not capitalized. We choose not to acknowledge him, even to the point of violating grammatical rules.

Treasure House

An Imprint of
Destiny Image® Publishers, Inc.

P.O. Box 310
Shippensburg, PA 17257-0310

"For where your treasure is,
there will your heart be also." Matthew 6:21

ISBN 1-56043-313-2

For Worldwide Distribution
Printed in the U.S.A.

This book and all other Destiny Image, Revival Press,
and Treasure House books are available
at Christian bookstores and distributors worldwide.

For a U.S. bookstore nearest you, call **1-800-722-6774**.
For more information on foreign distributors, call **717-532-3040**.
Or reach us on the Internet: **http://www.reapernet.com**

Dedication

This book is lovingly dedicated to a very special person who has stood by me, through thick and thin, for more than 27 years. No man could ever have a better friend than James W. Strickhausen. For me, Jim is the friend who has stuck closer than a brother. Thanks, Jim, for the memories. The best is yet to come!

Contents

Foreword

Chapter 1 The Truth About Holiness 1

Chapter 2 Three Tenses of Holiness 13

Chapter 3 Righteousness 25

Chapter 4 Disputable Matters 37

Chapter 5 True Repentance 57

Chapter 6 The Gift of Grace 67

Chapter 7 Life With the Spirit 79

Chapter 8 Walking in Holiness 95

Foreword

Dr. Hellmann has done an outstanding job in his new book, *False Holiness Exposed*, with its practical insights into the message of holiness. He shares how to apply it to your life in a day and age when there is so much condemnation and judgment preached along with the message of repentance. Many don't understand that it is the goodness of God that leads us to repentance, as Romans 2:1-4 shows.

Jesus did not come to the world to condemn the world. He came with love, acceptance, and forgiveness.

For God so loved the world, that He gave His only begotten Son, that whosoever believeth in Him should not perish, but have everlasting life. For God sent not His Son into the world to condemn the world; but that the world through Him might be saved (John 3:16-17 KJV).

Many serve God out of fear and then try to live the life of the Spirit in the flesh. God has a higher plan and purpose for the Church—the blood-bought, blood-washed children of the living God. It's a life of holiness without works, a relationship based on love and faith.

In this book you will see the difference between conviction and condemnation. In it you'll find the keys to the life of holiness. May you read it prayerfully and may the scales of religion and tradition fall from your eyes, so that you can see all that was purchased for you at Calvary.

Dr. Rodney M. Howard-Browne
Tampa, Florida

Chapter 1

The Truth About Holiness

And God blessed the seventh day and made it holy, because on it he rested from all the work of creating that he had done (Genesis 2:3).

This is the first time the word *holy* is used in the Bible. The first thing that was made holy was a day, the seventh day. This first usage of the word *holy* reveals to us one of its meanings. *Holy* basically describes something as separated unto God, consecrated to God, devoted to God, dedicated to God, and belonging to Him for His purposes and use. Holy means *special*.

The seventh day, or Sabbath day, was not to be like the previous six days. It was to be a special day, a sacred day, in a way that was unique from the other six. The first six days were common days, ordinary days. During these six days man was to get up, go to work, come home, and go to bed.

The seventh day, however, was to be different. It was to be unlike the other days. On the seventh day, man was not to get up, go to work, and live his usual routine. He was to devote his time on that day to the worship of the Lord. Because the seventh day was devoted to the worship of the Lord, it was a sacred day. Anything separated unto God becomes sacred.

What Is Holy?

In the Old Testament, God called Israel to be a "holy nation" (Ex. 19:6). In other words, out of all the nations of the world, Israel belonged to God in a special way. Israel was called out of the nations to belong to God for His plans. This calling made Israel a sacred nation, a holy nation. They were separated from the other nations of the world and set apart to be God's treasured possession.

The prophet Balaam said of the people of God, "I see them from the cliff tops; I watch them from the hills. I see a people who live by themselves, set apart from other nations" (Num. 23:9 NLT). Moses also instructed the people, "You have been set apart as holy to the Lord your God, and he has chosen you to be his own special treasure from all the nations of the earth" (Deut. 14:2 NLT). These two declarations confirm that *holy* means set apart from the common and belonging to God.

When God called Moses to meet with Him at the top of Mount Sinai, He gave Moses this command, "Put limits around the mountain and set it apart as holy" (Ex. 19:23b). The mountain was set apart as holy because God was going to use it. There was nothing in that mountain that made it different from any other mountain on the face of the earth. But because God was on that mountain and was going to use it, it became holy or special. It became a mountain that was set apart for God's special purpose. God's use of an object is what makes it holy, not the inherent qualities of the object itself.

Christians are struggling to be holy. They know that God is a holy, righteous God and that He has called us to be like Him (see Mt. 5:48). When Christians compare their lives and actions against God's moral law as it is laid out in His Word, they often find areas where they have fallen short. This is good because it shows us our need for a Savior. We cannot save ourselves as the humanists teach. Only Jesus can save us, and only Jesus can make us holy.

Do we really understand what it means to be holy? Do we understand what it means to be called out, set apart, and dedicated to God for His purposes and His use? Does God require that we each be sinless? Can we truly be righteous and holy before God?

The Word of God shows us that there are clearly such things as right and wrong. As Christians we live in the realm known as the Kingdom of God. In this Kingdom, we have laws of love and rules of order to live by that God outlines in the Scriptures. We know that we cannot accept Jesus Christ as our Lord and then live however we please. We must live His way.

As Christians, we have become a part of the people of God. We are His Church. We need to understand that the Greek word for "church," *ekklesia*, refers to the group of "called out ones." The Church is comprised of those people whom God has called out of the world, who have changed lords, and who have knowingly submitted their whole existence to the authority of Jesus Christ. Christians have been called out of the world and called to Jesus Christ. Our inward man and our outward behavior is to reflect that change.

God calls His people, "My holy people" (see Ex. 22:31). This phrase applies to those people whom God has set apart from all other people for His special purposes. They are sacred people, people who belong to God in a unique way. All the people in the world are God's, but this passage as well as others show that Israel is His in a very distinctive way. He has special plans to use Israel for His own intentions. Through the cross of Christ and the New Covenant, we as Christians can also count ourselves as part of the holy, set apart people of God.

In all these references it would be impossible for *holy* to mean sinless. How can a day of the week be sinless? How can a parcel of land, a nation, or a mountain be sinless?

Similarly, when Israel built the tabernacle it contained areas called the Holy Place and the Most Holy Place. Were the materials used to construct the Tabernacle sinless materials or were the materials set apart for the Presence of God? The wood and fabrics used to build the tabernacle were not going into an ox cart or a merchant's stand; they were going into a structure that God would use in a sacred way. God's purpose and presence made the tabernacle holy, and the wood and materials had nothing to do with it.

Holiness—Selected for God's Service

Your brother, Aaron, and his sons, Nadab, Abihu, Eleazar, and Ithamar, will be set apart from the common people. They will be my priests and will minister to me. Make special clothing for Aaron to show his separation to God... (Exodus 28:1-2 NLT).

In these verses, God reveals to us what holiness really is. Aaron and his sons were *set apart* from the common people. God set them apart, and it was this action of calling or setting apart that made them holy. Were Aaron and his sons any better than any of the other people? No. They were not better, but they were selected by God and separated unto God for His purpose, which in this case was the priesthood. It was this selection and separation that made them holy.

That's what true biblical holiness is: *separation unto God.* Were Aaron and his sons more pure and moral than the others? No. It was not any moral purity on their part that qualified them for the priesthood. It was the call and purpose of God for them that made them holy. Aaron had showed his sinful streak when he made the golden calf and led Israel in worshiping it. However, through this we can see that those whom God separates are holy because God has taken them out of the common for His purposes, not because they are ethically or morally perfect. Whatever is set apart from the common and is set apart to be God's special possession is holy. This includes you!

Set Apart Through Salvation

The call to salvation in Jesus Christ was the call to come out of the common people and be set apart unto God, to belong to Him and to His eternal plans and purposes (see Rom. 1:6). When addressing the church in Corinth, Paul wrote, "To the church of God in Corinth, to those sanctified in Christ Jesus and called to be holy..." (1 Cor. 1:2). Sanctified means "made holy." We are made holy in Christ Jesus, not in ourselves. Does being called to be holy mean that we are called to be sinless? No, it means called to be sacred—called out of the world, called to belong to God for His plans and purposes, called to be His special possession.

The Lord Jesus spoke to Paul concerning the Gentiles, "Then they will receive forgiveness for their sins and be given a place among God's people, who are set apart by faith in me" (Acts 26:18b NLT). It is by our faith in Jesus Christ that we are set apart as holy to the Lord, not our goodness or attempts at sinless perfection. Our faith in the Redeemer sets us apart and makes us holy in God's sight.

Think about it: There are over six billion people currently alive on this earth, yet you and I are special to God. He has called us out of the great mass of humanity to belong to Himself. He has plans and purposes for each of us. We are as special to Him as Israel is. We are set apart to Him, just like Aaron was. We have been called out to belong to Him by His grace—not because of anything we have done. We don't deserve to be called out. We don't deserve to belong to Him. He did the selecting and choosing, and He chose you! If you are born again, you are not a common, ordinary person. You are no longer of this world. You have been called out of this world as a special person with a divine purpose.

Imagine a large sandpile. Think of the billions and billions of individual grains of sand in that sandpile. Now imagine a person going over to that pile of sand and carefully selecting some individual grains, plucking them out of the pile with his fingers. As the person takes these carefully hand-picked grains of sand and walks away from the huge sandpile, he is separating some of the grains from the billions and billions of other grains. The sandpile is still there, but some individual grains are missing. Now the person who took the grains of sand out of the sandpile is free to build something that he wants from the sand he has selected. That is exactly what it means to be holy! God has come and separated us from the mass of humanity for His purposes, and He is building His Church.

You did not separate yourself from the world and the rest of humanity. God separated you. It was all God! What made Him select you? Grace! Grace! Grace! His unearned and undeserved favor. You were selected by God. That act of separation is called holiness! God made you holy by calling you to salvation. Your part in holiness was that you responded positively when God called. You answered the call. It is because of God and the work of Jesus Christ that you are now a holy person. You have now become separated from the common mass of humanity because God has a plan to use you for His glory. You are special! Think of the billions of others who may not have been called. Think of the ones who were called but who rejected it. Yet by the grace of God you answered, and you are holy.

When Paul wrote to the Corinthians regarding a marriage between a believer to an unbeliever, he said, "For the unbelieving husband has been sanctified through his wife, and the unbelieving wife has been sanctified through her believing husband. Otherwise your children would be unclean, but as it is, they are holy" (1 Cor. 7:14). Are these children sinless? Are they perfect? No. That is not what the Bible means because holy does not mean sinless or perfect.

Paul is explaining that these children are sacred and not common. They belong to God and not to the world. The children are not made unacceptable to God because of the spiritual state of the unbelieving parent. Instead, because of God's grace, they are made holy and acceptable because of the faith of the believing parent.

False Holiness

Mankind is so negative. We have made holiness a negative thing. We have defined it to mean successfully avoiding anything that we're "not supposed to do." How shallow it is to think that holiness is not watching TV or not going to the movies. How ridiculous it is to think that true biblical holiness is "not wearing makeup or a nice dress." To most religious people, holiness is nothing more than a long list of "thou shalt nots." We've made God's beautiful holiness into an ugly thing. We've created a list of rules and laws and said, "If you don't do these things you are holy." How absurd!

Man is more interested in superficial holiness than the true holiness of the heart. The Bible reveals the true holiness of God. Religious man has created his own definition of holiness, and it is often quite different from God's holiness. Some people are transfixed by man's form of holiness and think it is wonderful. But it is nothing more than what I call "hyper-holiness." Hyper-holiness is false holiness, or man's holiness that is taken to extremes.

False holiness often comes from a man preaching his own conscience as the Word of God, telling everyone that everything is a sin. He may be telling everyone else to measure up to his own personal standard, a standard that cannot be supported by any chapter or verse of Scripture. Over the years, I have learned that those who preach this hyper-holiness message can be using it as a cover to hide their own sins. It can also be the means that a guilty person uses in an attempt to atone for his own wretchedness. When people are in a grave struggle with sin they may very well go to the opposite extreme and preach hyper-holiness in order to feel better about themselves. However, real holiness is something wonderful God has done for you. It's not something you do for God.

Our holiness is not dependent upon our personal perfection in our thoughts and behavior. Consider the prophets of the Old Testament. The apostle Peter referred to them as the "holy prophets" (see Acts 3:21). Were the prophets people who were without sin or fault? No. They were as sinful as you or I, but they were men who belonged to God and were separated to Him for His purposes and that made them holy. Isaiah knew that he was a sinner and far from perfect. When God called him, his first response was an immediate awareness of his own depravity. He cried out, "Woe to me!...I am ruined! For I am a man of unclean lips, and I live among a people of unclean lips..." (Is. 6:5). Yet God divinely purified him and used him for His purposes, just as the work of Jesus purifies us for the service of His Kingdom.

Because we are sacred people, we are to live in this world and conduct ourselves as people of God. We are to abstain from sin and forms of uncleanness wherever they may be found. The Bible contains many exhortations concerning the conduct of God's people—whom He has made special and set apart. Consider the following example:

But among you there must not be even a hint of sexual immorality, or of any kind of impurity, or of greed, because these are improper for God's holy people (Ephesians 5:3).

We are to be holy as God is holy (see 1 Pet. 1:16). We are to be as separated as He is. But God makes us holy first, and then we live it. We don't live it as part of any effort to be made holy.

Purity Apart from Christ

I am going to make a statement here that may be the direct opposite of everything you have ever heard about holiness: *Moral purity alone does not make anyone holy.*

Stop and think about that for a few minutes. If moral purity is holiness, then the Muslims are the most holy people on the earth. In fact, they will not allow Western television to be broadcast in their countries because of all the lifestyles and acts of sex, drugs, and alcohol shown in the movies and television shows. In Islamic nations, things such as adultery are considered crimes. If someone is caught stealing, he may have his hand cut off as punishment. Muslim nations have strong doctrines against our Western vices, and their people abide by a very strict "moral" conduct. Are they holy? Does their impeccable morality make them God's holy people? No! They are not set apart to the true God of the Bible, and they do not recognize Jesus Christ as their Lord. Strict religious morality is not God's holiness. Holiness is not moral perfection; rather, it is separation to the true God.

God makes us holy, and then we apply His holiness to the way we live. If God has called you and separated you unto Himself, you must live right. God has provided guidance for you in His Word and through His Holy Spirit. If you do not choose to live rightly, you will grieve God by transgressing against Him. Sin will interfere with your relationship with Him. It can keep you from fulfilling His plans for your life. He presents principles and rules in Scripture for your benefit and to help you be successful. If you transgress His moral law, you will also bring a ton of misery upon yourself. Flee from sin!

In the Scriptures we are told, "But just as he who called you is holy, so be holy in all you do; for it is written, 'Be holy, because I am holy'" (1 Pet. 1:15-16). We who are holy cannot live unclean lives or participate in unclean things. We are to be separated from the world and its unclean practices. We are also to be separate and different from the unclean people of the world. We are to follow the example that Jesus set for us:

> *He is the kind of high priest we need because he is holy and blameless, unstained by sin. He has now been set apart from sinners, and he has been given the highest place of honor in heaven* (Hebrews 7:26 NLT).

To be holy as God is holy certainly includes being separated from the sinful people of this world and the sin and uncleanness in which they indulge. We must be around sinners, but we cannot be like them. We may be among them, but we cannot imitate them or live as they do. We are special, so let's act it! Let's bring praise to God by our lives and by the way in which we handle things. Our lives need to show forth the light and life of Christ in this sin-darkened world. May our actions draw people to the light within us so that we can share the good news of Jesus Christ with them.

Thanks be to God who has called us and separated us to Himself! We belong to Him, for we were bought at a high price—the price of His own Son, Jesus Christ. Since He has purchased us and made us holy, let us therefore honor God with our bodies and with the way we live (see 1 Cor. 6:20).

Chapter 2

Three Tenses of Holiness

Studying the topic of holiness in the Bible can be very confusing. Listening to different preachers as they discuss holiness can be equally as confusing. One person may preach holiness as though we have already been made holy. Another reputable man will say, "No, we must strive to be holy." And still another will declare, "We won't really be holy until Jesus returns and our bodies are gloriously changed." So, who is right? *They all are!* That's because there is a past tense holiness, a present tense holiness, and a future tense holiness. The Bible speaks of holiness in all three tenses. Let's take a closer look at what the Bible has to say about the different tenses of holiness.

Past Tense Holiness

Then he said, "Here I am, I have come to do your will." He sets aside the first to establish the second.

And by that will, we have been made holy through the sacrifice of the body of Jesus Christ once for all (Hebrews 10:9-10).

And so Jesus also suffered outside the city gate to make the people holy through His own blood (Hebrews 13:12).

The Scriptures make it absolutely clear that we have been made holy through the sacrifice and blood of Jesus Christ. Our holiness *was* taken care of by Jesus on the cross. His blood not only makes the vilest sinner clean; it also makes the vilest sinner holy and righteous before God. As believers, we have already been made holy. We are holy and righteous at this very minute. Even while we are struggling against sin, we are holy. We did not make ourselves holy; Christ made us holy. I don't have to worry about holiness. It's in His blood!

You need to accept this great gospel truth by faith and begin to change your self-image. See yourself as a holy person. Begin to change the way you talk about yourself. Quit talking like a sinner. Talk like a holy man or woman of God. You cannot make yourself holy. Christ has already made you holy! Believe that. Believe the written Word of God. Believe in the power of His blood. If the Word of God declares you to be holy, then it is so. God's Word is true. Don't doubt it.

Many preachers who preach on holiness ignore the truth that Jesus has already made His people holy. To disbelieve or to neglect this truth is to deny the blood of Jesus. The blood of Jesus has made us holy. The blood of Jesus is our *only* hope.

Some pastors preach on holiness and try to persuade us that we must become obsessed with working on ourselves until we get all sin out of our lives. They present a list of rules and tell us that our holiness depends on keeping those rules. They declare that once we have removed all sin from our lives and are living according to the correct standards, that we will then be holy. However, because of the blood of Jesus, we're already holy. We're not sinless or perfect. But we *are* holy. We are separated unto God.

The holiness that comes to us through the blood of Jesus is the past tense holiness that the faith movement has preached. People within that movement have emphasized the past tense holiness brought to us by the death of Christ, and this is a wonderful biblical truth. However, if this is the *only* "tense" of holiness that you preach, people will feel as if they can live any way they please because they are already holy through the blood. Many Charismatic churches are hotbeds of sin because of this type of teaching. People are resting on the finished work of Christ while living like the devil. Some individuals are living immorally, addicted to drugs, cheating in their business, and cussing like sailors throughout the week. But when they come to church on Sunday, they sing, shout, and dance and think that all is well. However, all is *not* well. Our congregations need to hear the whole Word of God preached and not just part of it. "Past tense" holiness must be preached, but that is not all the Bible has to say on the subject.

Traditional Pentecostals often preached "present tense" holiness, while completely ignoring "past tense" holiness. As a result, many people became negatively introspective, always looking for sin within themselves. Ignoring the truth of the holiness that comes to us through the sacrifice of Christ will keep people in chronic guilt, condemnation, and repentance. Our walk with God should not be one of habitual repentance and telling God that we are no good. How can we experience the joy of the Lord and His salvation when we are constantly groveling before Him and examining ourselves for even the slightest defect? How can you live a life of peace when you are always on your face before God telling Him what a piece of garbage you are? Surely, God does not want us to live like that. Surely, that is not the life that Christ died for.

What we desperately need on this subject is balance, balance, balance! Any truth taken to an extreme creates a warped people. Even holiness taken to an extreme can become an error. Every biblical truth must be balanced with other biblical truths. It is possible for us to go to seed on any one biblical topic and be preaching error before we know it. Many times error is simply the absence of balance.

The absence of teaching on the holiness that comes through the blood of Christ creates negative people who live in condemnation, harshly judge others, and have no joy, peace, or self-esteem. Overemphasis on past tense holiness without addressing the need for present tense development of holiness in our character creates people who rest on the grace of God and live ungodly lives. Both teachings are incomplete when separated from each other.

Although we are completely holy in God's sight because of the blood of Jesus, we still need to work on perfecting our character. This perfecting of our character is "present tense" holiness.

Present Tense Holiness

Thanks be to the Father that the death, burial, and resurrection of Jesus Christ has totally set us apart from the world, sin, and uncleanness. Because of His sacrifice the New Testament calls the born-again believer, a saint!

To all in Rome who are loved by God and called to be saints... (Romans 1:7).

In the eyes of the Father, the blood of His Son has already turned every Christian from a sinner into a saint. The problem is that we don't act like saints. Tragically, more times than not, we act like sinners. The way we live in this world should match who we are in the courts of Heaven. *Saints shouldn't live like sinners.*

The perfection and holiness that we have been given through Christ is wonderful, but our character is still under construction and needs plenty of work. It is a biblical truth that we are presently "being made holy."

*But when this priest had offered for all time one sacrifice for sins, he sat down at the right hand of God. Since that time he waits for his enemies to be made his footstool, because by one sacrifice he has made perfect forever **those who are being made holy*** (Hebrews 10:12-14).

The same Book of Hebrews that declares that Christ has made us holy also declares that there is a present-day process whereby we are being made holy. We find this truth in other Scriptures as well. Consider, for example, Romans 15:16:

...a minister of Christ Jesus to the Gentiles with the priestly duty of proclaiming the gospel of God, so that the Gentiles might become an offering acceptable to God, sanctified by the Holy Spirit.

There is a sanctification, separation, and development of our character that can only come through a relationship with the Holy Spirit. The blood has made us holy, but there is yet another dimension of holiness. The Holy Spirit helps us to become holy as we live for Christ in this world. Who is better equipped to teach us holiness than the *Holy* Spirit?

Sanctification by the Spirit

Walking with the Holy Spirit is marvelous. He is my personal friend. He is so kind, patient, and gentle with me. He is also long-suffering toward me. I met Jesus Christ in 1966. I didn't meet the Person of the Holy Spirit until 1995. I can testify that since I have come to know the Holy Spirit, He has definitely made me more holy in every area of my life. And He is not through with me yet!

The Holy Spirit helps us to overcome every sin in our hearts and lives. Right now, millions of God's people are in the situation that I was in from 1966 to 1995. They know Jesus, but they don't personally know the Helper, the Comforter, the Advocate, the Intercessor—the Holy Spirit. How have we missed verses of Scripture such as, "For if you live according to the sinful nature, you will die; but if by the *Spirit* you put to death the misdeeds of the body, you will live" (Rom. 8:13)?

The Holy Spirit is the key to present tense holiness. We can only put sin to death by the Holy Spirit or with the help and power of the Holy Spirit. You can do nothing without the Spirit. Will power has shown itself to be miserably inadequate in restraining the flesh and stopping sin. The Holy Spirit stops sin as it tries to operate in us and through us. We can't stop sin on our own. Every time that we've tried, we've failed. In Romans 7, Paul talks about his failure at stopping sin by his own power and ability:

I know that nothing good lives in me, that is, in my sinful nature. For I have the desire to do what is good, but I cannot carry it out. For what I do is not the good I want to do; no, the evil I do not want to do—this I keep on doing. Now if I do what I do not want to do, it is no longer I who do it, but it is sin living in me that does it (Romans 7:18-20).

Very few people have the resolve and will power to crush sin and bad habits. The relatively few who do succeed often do so because they have been threatened with physical death. Many persons have quit smoking only after a physician told them that if they didn't stop, they would die.

Sin in us is overcome by close, intimate relationship and fellowship with the Holy Spirit. When He truly fills us and takes over every area in our lives, then sin, addiction, and bad habits must move out. And when they move out, it is because He is forcing them out, not because we are doing so.

We are being made holy by the Holy Spirit. You have no sin, iniquity, rebellion, addiction, or habit that He cannot and will not destroy. He is the key! Get filled with the Spirit and live filled with the Spirit, and you will find that the power of sin is no match for Him. We overcome sin, not by our might and not by our human power, but by the Spirit (see Zech. 4:6). We are being sanctified by the Person of the

Holy Spirit. The blood of Jesus *has already* made us holy. The Holy Spirit *is making* us holy!

Sanctification by the Word of God

There is also a purity that comes to us "...by the washing with water through the word" (Eph. 5:26). The written Word of God separates us and changes us as we read it, study it, and apply it to our lives.

How can a young man keep his way pure? By living according to your word (Psalm 119:9).

The written Word of God contains the power of God. The power of God within the Word changes our lives from faith to faith. When we take in the Word, God's power goes to work on our minds, emotions, and wills. It changes our thinking and our conduct. The Word of God forms the nature of God within us. It builds God's character into our character. The more of the Word that we know and practice the more we will live the life of a saint. God's Word has awesome, life-changing power. So, we can correctly say that we are being made holy by the written Word of God. The Scriptures speak of "...the word of God, which is at work in you who believe" (1 Thess. 2:13). The Word of God works within us to make us holy.

When Jesus was praying in John 17:17, He said, "Sanctify them by the truth; your word is truth." *Sanctify* means to make holy. The truth makes us holy, and the Word of God is truth. The more of the Word that we know and practice, the holier we will become. Jesus also said, "I am the way and the truth and the life..." (Jn. 14:6). The truth of the Word helps to develop Christ's nature within believers to make us more holy and more like Christ. Those who refuse to expose themselves to the Word will not grow and develop. The written Word is essential if we are to be holy like He is holy.

Obedience and Self-Examination

But in a great house there are not only vessels of gold and of silver, but also of wood and of earth; and some to honour, and some to dishonour. If a man therefore purge himself from these, he shall be a vessel unto honour, sanctified, and meet for the master's use, and prepared unto every good work (2 Timothy 2:20-21 KJV).

The Bible is a book of balance. Although God cleanses us from sin, we need to cleanse ourselves from other things. We do have a role to play. We must be filled with the Spirit, yield to Him, and allow Him to take things away from us and out of us. We must not resist the working of the Spirit or the written Word. We must submit to it with a willing and obedient heart. Pray, yield, take a good look at yourself. Do not examine yourself by any set of man-made rules or standards, but by the Word and your own conscience. Remember, sin of any kind brings misery and unhappiness. If you have chronic misery, bare your heart to God and see if you are participating in any form of sin.

It is good and healthy to periodically take stock of yourself and make amends wherever necessary. Stop some things that you should not be doing. Start other things you should be doing. Change your mind about some issues. Lay your heart and your life before the Lord and ask Him to remove anything that is not pleasing in His sight. Examine your heart, attitudes, and motives. Make things right with other people. Make sure no bitterness or unforgiveness is growing in your heart.

"Make every effort to live in peace with all men and to be holy; without holiness no one will see the Lord" (Heb. 12:14). "Make every effort" to be holy. This proves that there is a realm of holiness that requires our effort to attain. We must work toward it.

Jesus has already made us holy, but holiness doesn't stop there. While we are all on this earth, we are each working on ourselves with the Lord. We will not be perfect in this life, but we are being perfected. We are being made into His image and likeness. He is working on our character and personality. It's not right to say, "Christ has made me holy," and then go on to lie, cheat, steal, swear, become drunk, hit your spouse, and live like a lost sinner. Anyone with any sense knows that living like that is not right and does not please the Lord or make the Lord and His salvation look good to other people.

The Bible teaches us to live in such a way as to make the teaching about God our Savior attractive (see Tit. 2:10). Some hate their job, slander the boss, arrive late, leave early, take pens and paper from the office, gripe constantly, laugh at dirty jokes, and then invite everyone in the office to church. If you are going to live like that you should at least uphold the name of the Lord by not telling anyone that you are a Christian. That way God's name will not be blasphemed among the unbelievers by the way you live (see Rom. 2:24).

Yes, Jesus has already made us holy, but we are being made holy too.

future Tense Holiness

Holiness is "past tense," "present tense," and "future tense." There is a holiness that is already ours; a holiness that we are working on right now; and a holiness that will be completed in us when we go to Heaven.

*May he strengthen your hearts **so that you will be** blameless and holy in the presence of our God and Father when our Lord Jesus comes with all his holy ones* (1 Thessalonians 3:13).

This holiness is a process that won't be fully complete until the Lord Jesus comes. When He comes, however, in a moment, in the twinkling of an eye, we will be completely holy!

As much as I try to co-operate with the Lord as He works on me, there are still times when I fail. But even then I can always look ahead, by faith, knowing that one day the full transformation will be completed in a moment by His power. There is no doubt about it. In this matter of sin and holiness, I will ultimately win because of Jesus!

Because holiness is a process, there are past tense, present tense, and future tense applications of holiness in our lives. In the past tense, Jesus has already made us holy. In the present tense, we are working with God as He forms His likeness into us. Yet there is still a future tense, for the day will come when God will work supernaturally and change our vile bodies to be like His glorious body.

Thank God He is not through with us. We're on a journey that is not yet finished. And, as I have already stated, in this matter of holiness, we will win because of Jesus!

Chapter 3

Righteousness

The word *gospel* means "good news." When the true gospel of Jesus Christ is being proclaimed, it is good news that is being proclaimed. The gospel is not the law. Many people have an incorrect understanding of Christianity and the gospel. The gospel of Jesus is not one "thou shalt not" after another—the law is. The gospel is the good news concerning Jesus Christ. More precisely, it is what Jesus Christ has done for every person through His death, burial, and resurrection.

Two great books in the New Testament focus on the theme of righteousness. They teach us how an unholy, unrighteous human being can be made holy and righteous in the sight of an awesome God. The two books I am referring to are Paul's Epistles to the Romans and the Galatians. Every born-again believer must immerse himself in the great truths taught in these two books. Without being rooted and grounded in the basic teaching of righteousness that is presented in Romans and Galatians, believers can easily fall prey to error and legalistic righteousness.

Righteousness Comes by Faith

> *For in the gospel a righteousness from God is revealed, a righteousness that is by faith from first to last, just as it is written: "The righteous will live by faith"* (Romans 1:17).

The gospel is the good news of how we can be made absolutely righteous in the sight of God! In this verse we get our first glimpse of this brand-new way to be made righteous—through *faith*. Notice the phrase, "a righteousness that is by faith." This is not a righteousness that comes by law. This is not a righteousness that comes by being good. This is not a righteousness that comes by doing the right thing, nor can it be obtained from abstaining from acts of sin. It is not a righteousness that we earn by being religious. This righteousness cannot be attained by spending hours in prayer or hours in Bible study. Going to church will not bring this righteousness. Tithing, soul-winning, taking care of orphans, and supplying food and shelter to the homeless will not give you this righteousness and make you acceptable to God. To the contrary, this righteousness *only comes by faith in what Jesus has done for you!*

The righteousness that the Bible teaches cannot be bought, earned, or merited in any way, by anyone.

Mother Teresa died in the fall of 1997. She was a Nobel prize winner and was admired worldwide for her work among the poorest of the poor in India. Mother Teresa did many, many great works, there is no doubt about it. But nothing on her list of accomplishments and good deeds made her righteous and acceptable in God's sight. Mother Teresa's ministry to the poor did not qualify her for Heaven. Ministering to the poor cannot get anyone into Heaven. Mother Teresa's long hours of prayer and sacrifice of all material possessions could not and did not get her into Heaven. Mother Teresa is now in Heaven because of one thing and one thing alone, and it is the same thing that will get you into Heaven. Mother Teresa believed in Jesus! She believed in His death on the cross for her sins. She believed in Jesus' burial and in His literal, physical resurrection. In other words, Mother Teresa believed the gospel.

Many years ago Mother Teresa first believed that Jesus died on the cross for her—personally. The moment that she chose to believe the gospel of Jesus, she was declared righteous by God. Over the years when Mother Teresa was working among the poor, she was working, not to become righteous, but because she was already righteous. She was not working to earn a place in Heaven. She was working because she was already a citizen of Heaven through the death of Christ. It was only Mother Teresa's faith in the redemptive work of the Son of God that opened a way into Heaven for her. That's the only way any of us can go to Heaven. There is *no* other way.

Righteousness comes by faith in Jesus—not by works, not by being good, not by doing right. Righteousness is yours the instant that you believe in Jesus as your personal Lord and Savior. At that moment you receive the holiness and righteousness of Jesus Christ and you begin the process of being transformed into His holy likeness.

The Law Points to the Cross

Romans 3:20-22 continues the theme of a righteousness that can only come to you by your faith in Jesus and His work on the cross:

Therefore no one will be declared righteous in his sight by observing the law; rather, through the law we become conscious of sin. But now a righteousness from God, apart from law, has been made known, to which the Law and the Prophets testify. This righteousness from God comes through faith in Jesus Christ to all who believe....

No one will be declared righteous in God's sight by obeying the Ten Commandments or any other commandments. Obeying commandments cannot and does not make us righteous. In other words, being good, or being what we call a "good person," does not get anyone into Heaven. Most people think that if they are good enough they will go to Heaven. That is an absolute lie. In fact, many people hold to an erroneous theology that states that good people go to Heaven and bad people go to hell. Again, this implies that our goodness can cause us to *deserve* Heaven. That is not true. No matter how good you are or how good you try to be, your goodness will never be enough to qualify you for Heaven or make you acceptable to God. Faith in Jesus Christ, God's Son, is the only thing that makes you acceptable to God. But because of your faith God Himself has declared you to be righteous. New Testament righteousness had nothing to do with your achievements or works; it has everything to do with Jesus Christ.

A number of years ago a wonderful lady attended my church. She was always doing kind things for other people. She was the most benevolent person I had ever met. She would take food to the local Teen Challenge ministry and feed everyone present. She housed strangers and took clothes to the poor. She was always doing this type of work. I thought that she was perhaps the most Christ-like person I had ever met. Then, one night, actually in the middle of the night, this lady got on her bicycle and rode to a friend's house. She rang the doorbell in the pitch blackness of night. When the door was opened, she burst inside and said, "I can't take it any longer. Tell me how to be saved!"

All the good deeds that this woman had done were her attempts to merit eternal life. But no matter how many good deeds she performed, she remained dead on the inside. When she stopped working to earn salvation and believed in Jesus and what He had already done for her, she found peace and true righteousness. Now she was free to do good *because* she was righteous, not in order to become righteous.

Simply put, you can't *do* anything to get into Heaven. There is no deed or lifetime of deeds that will open the gates of Heaven to you. If you single-handedly led every human being in the world to Christ and you were depending on that to make you righteous, you would utterly fail and spend eternity in hell. If you personally fed every hungry boy and girl in the whole world and you were trusting in that deed to get your soul into Heaven, you would go straight to hell. If you bought and delivered clothes to every man, woman, and child in the world who needed clothing and you thought, *Surely that will get me into Heaven*, you would be dead wrong and your soul would still spend eternity in hell.

What are you depending on to make you righteous? What are you counting on to get you into Heaven? What right do you have to go to Heaven? What are you trusting to be your ticket into glory? If the answer to these questions is anything other than Jesus, His death, and His blood, you are deceived and bound for hell. You may be good, but you will still go to hell. Good people go to hell every second of every minute of every day.

Jesus Christ, Not Religion

Just as goodness cannot save you, neither can religion. You can believe in God and go to hell. Belief in the existence of God is not the faith that saves. You could believe in God as your Creator and still go to hell.

> *At Caesarea there was a man named Cornelius, a centurion in what was known as the Italian Regiment. He and all his family were devout and God-fearing; he gave generously to those in need and prayed to God regularly* (Acts 10:1-2).

Cornelius was a man like many in our day. He believed in the existence of God. He was devoutly religious. He gave money. He prayed frequently. And, he was lost, unsaved, and bound for hell. This is proof that a good person or a religious person is not necessarily a saved person. Goodness cannot save. Religion cannot save. When Cornelius heard the gospel of Jesus Christ, he believed immediately and received the salvation and righteousness for which he had been longing.

Prayer doesn't save; Jesus saves. Fasting doesn't save; Jesus saves. Church doesn't save; Jesus saves. Giving doesn't save; Jesus saves. Being good doesn't save; Jesus saves. Obeying moral laws doesn't save; Jesus saves. Obeying religious laws doesn't save; Jesus saves. Trying to make yourself holy doesn't save; Jesus saves. Denominational rules don't save; Jesus saves. Your own rules don't save; only Jesus saves.

The Father of Faith

Although the righteousness that comes by faith is a New Testament concept, this all-important truth goes all the way back to Abraham. Abraham was the first person to experience being made righteous by his faith in God. Romans 4:3 says, "...Abraham believed God, and it was credited to him as righteousness."

Abraham was worried because he was old and had no heir. He and Sarah wanted their own son, but for many years they were unable to have a child. But God kept promising Abraham that he and Sarah would have a son of their very own. On one occasion, Abraham thought that Eliezer of Damascus, his servant, was going to be his heir. When he talked to God about this, God responded,

> ..."This man will not be your heir, but a son coming from your own body will be your heir." He took him outside and said, "Look up at the heavens and count the stars—if indeed you can count them." Then he said to him, "So shall your offspring be." Abram believed the Lord, and he credited it to him as righteousnesss (Genesis 15:4-6).

Abraham did not do anything to be made righteous in God's sight. So it was not what Abraham did that made him righteous. It was what he believed that made him righteous. And what did Abraham believe? He believed God. He believed what God said concerning the birth of a son. He believed God against all odds. He took God at His word. When he believed what God told him, God took the initiative and declared Abraham righteous. The Bible states it this way, "...and he [God] credited it [Abraham's faith] to him as righteousness" (Gen. 15:6).

In these days, the faith that is credited to you as righteousness is the faith you have in Jesus Christ as your Lord and Savior. When you, by the grace of God, put your trust in Jesus and His death, God declares you to be righteous. Your faith is credited to you as righteousness.

Christ Alone

Once the crowd asked Jesus, "What must we do to do the works God requires?" Jesus responded, "The work of God is this: to believe in the one he has sent" (Jn. 6:28-29). That was a revolutionary answer because the people in the crowd were accustomed to being given a long list of righteous deeds that they had to perform in order to merit eternal life.

Teaching Sunday school, being baptized, spending time in prayer, and even saving someone's life are all good things to do, but none of them will make you righteous. They do not make you right with God or acceptable to Him. You cannot do anything to be made acceptable to God. You can only believe what God has said about His Son, and if you believe what God has said about Jesus Christ, then you too will be declared righteous and will spend eternity in Heaven with Him!

You may also be saying, "But, but, but...I'm not worthy to go to Heaven. I don't deserve to go." You are right! None of us is worthy in ourselves. None of us deserves to go to Heaven. We will not go to Heaven because we are worthy and deserve to go. We will go because there is a God in Heaven who loves us and sent His Son to take our death and punishment for sin. We will go because the Son of God did a work for us on the cross by giving His life as a sacrifice for our sins. Someone else has done the work to get us into Heaven and make us righteous. Therefore we must trust in Jesus and His work: His death on the cross, His burial, and His resurrection. The only work that can get you into Heaven is the work Jesus has done for you.

However, to the man who does not work but trusts God who justifies the wicked, his faith is credited as righteousness. David says the same thing when he speaks of the blessedness of the man to whom God credits righteousness apart from works (Romans 4:5-6).

The Bible has many verses that talk about the righteousness that is credited to us by faith in Jesus Christ. It is difficult not to include scores and scores of them in this text. Let's look at just a few more.

The Scriptures declare, "Since they did not know the righteousness that comes from God and sought to establish their own, they did not submit to God's righteousness" (Rom. 10:3). Although this verse is specifically referring to Israel, it could be spoken about billions of people around the world, including many who claim to be Christian. I want you to notice three simple truths in this verse: First, people do not know the righteousness that comes from God; second, because people do not know about the righteousness that God gives them, they set out to establish their own righteousness; and third, these people are not submitting to God's righteousness or God's way of bringing righteousness to a person.

Most people, including Christians, want to earn their righteousness. Earning something gives us a feeling of accomplishment. It makes us feel worthy of the thing we have worked for. We feel we deserve it because we have worked for it. We have done something to attain it. This is the way of the man of the world, but it is the opposite of God's way.

When you come to God, you must be poor in spirit (see Mt. 5:3). You have to be so spiritually bankrupt in your own eyes that you know there is absolutely nothing you could ever do to earn God's love or favor. You must have the knowledge that you, of yourself, are totally depraved and totally and completely helpless to save yourself. There is nothing that you can do. This part of the gospel rubs many people the wrong way.

As people of the latter part of the twentieth century, we don't like to admit that we are helpless. Our pride won't allow us to make that acknowledgment. After all, we've put a man on the moon, we have wiped out entire diseases, we have planted new hearts in people's chests, and we are currently involved in a technological explosion that will take us to new heights in the coming millennium. Helpless? Not us, never.

That's why it's difficult for people to get truly born again in our day and age. We are so filled with self. We want man's salvation, not Jesus' salvation. We are self-righteous and are therefore unable to receive God's righteousness. We demand salvation and righteousness our way. The theme song of an old television show states man's attitude very clearly. The lyrics declared, "We'll do it our way, yes, our way, making our dreams come true...."

Scripture is very clear: When it comes to God and the things of God, our way has to die! We won't get anywhere doing things "our" way. We must do things "His" way. It's "His" way or no way at all. (See Psalm 127:1-2 and First Corinthians 3:11-14.)

Christ is the end of the law so that there may be righteousness for everyone who believes. Moses describes in this way the righteousness that is by the law: "The man who does these things will live by them." But the righteousness that is by faith says: "Do not say in your heart, 'Who will ascend into heaven?'" (that is, to bring Christ down) "or 'Who will descend into the deep?'" (that is, to bring Christ up from the dead). But what does it say? "The word is near you; it is in your mouth and in your heart," that is, the word of faith we are proclaiming: That if you confess with your mouth, "Jesus is Lord," and believe in your heart that God raised him from the dead, you will be saved. For it is with your heart that you believe and are justified [righteousness, KJV], and it is with your mouth that you confess and are saved (Romans 10:4-10).

Notice these points: First, Christ put an end to the law as a means of attaining righteousness; second, the Bible speaks of the righteousness that is by the law and the righteousness that is by faith, and we are called to the latter; and third, it is with your heart that you *believe* and are made righteous.

He saved us, not because of righteous things we had done, but because of his mercy. He saved us through the washing of rebirth and renewal by the Holy Spirit (Titus 3:5).

Righteousness comes by believing, not by doing or by abstaining.

It is because of him that you are in Christ Jesus, who has become for us wisdom from God—that is, our righteousness, holiness and redemption (1 Corinthians 1:30).

Christ is our righteousness. He is our holiness. Not one of us may dare to approach God in our own righteousness or holiness. Jesus is the Lord of our righteousness. He is the Lord of our holiness.

God made him who had no sin to be sin for us, so that in him we might become the righteousness of God (2 Corinthians 5:21).

Jesus took our sins and gave us His righteousness. We took His righteousness and gave Him our sins. It's called "the Great Exchange." On the cross an exchange was made: My sins went upon Him, and His righteousness came on me. Only the love of God could do something this great!

My friend, rely on the work of Christ and not on your own work. Trust the righteousness of Christ and not your own righteousness.

Righteousness, like salvation, is of the Lord from beginning to end. Our righteousness comes to us as a free gift of God's grace. Treasure it. Keep it ever before you. To "fall from grace" means that after trusting the atoning work of Christ for your salvation and righteousness, you have begun to trust your own good deeds. Trust Jesus, not yourself!

The only work you can do that will make you righteous and get you into Heaven is this: "Believe in the one the Father has sent" (see Jn. 6:29). The One whom the Father has sent is not Mohammed, Buddha, or Confucius. *Jesus Christ* is the One whom the Father has sent. Jesus is our righteousness!

Chapter 4

Disputable Matters

Accept him whose faith is weak, without passing judgment on disputable matters (Romans 14:1).

Many times we try to define righteousness and holiness in our own terms and try to force our opinions on others as biblical truth. As Christians, many of us are guilty of trying to judge someone else's standing with the Lord or rejecting him upon the basis of our personal ideas. However, in this issue of right and wrong, there is a gray area that includes all those things I like to call *disputable matters*. A disputable matter is any activity that is not specifically named in the Bible and for which we have no chapter and verse to define whether it is right or wrong. Watching television or going to the movies fall into this category. Although we do have a number of scriptural principles to guide us with these things, they are not specifically named in the Bible, and we have no chapter and verse that approves or condemns them. So, can a Christian go to the movies without sinning? Let's look at the truth of God as revealed in Romans 14.

"Accept him whose faith is weak" (Rom. 14:1a). As brothers and sisters in the house of God, God wants us to accept one another and not reject one another. God is concerned about our attitude toward other Christians. He wants us to be accepting of others, especially with regard to this area of disputable matters. To be on the receiving end of harsh rejection is very painful and hurtful. When people reject you, they basically wad you up like a piece of paper and throw you away as though you were worthless and no good. And we of the Body of Christ have certainly not learned how to disagree with one another in a loving way. To many, disagreement means a breaking of relationship and fellowship. This is absolutely tragic. We can disagree and still be close friends and have sweet fellowship together. God wants us to accept and not reject one another!

Don't throw away people for whom Christ died. If someone disagrees with your doctrine or your stand on an issue, is this a sufficient reason for discarding him as though he was a piece of trash? Definitely not. Even if you are right and the person you disagree with is wrong, will you be able to have a godly, positive influence on him by distancing yourself from him? No! To change someone's life you must be his friend. Jesus proved this. Do you think for a minute that the Lord Jesus approved of everything that His "sinner" friends did? Absolutely not. But He was still their friend, and He still fellowshiped with them. The sick need a doctor, but if the doctor will not come near, how can he treat the person and his illness?

Whose Righteousness?

I have loved and treasured the Lord for over 30 years and I am deeply spiritual, but I am not very religious—there is a difference. This was evidenced by the way my wife and I chose to celebrate our twenty-fifth wedding anniversary. We had spent most of our lives in the southeast, and we wanted to travel west to see a brand-new place. Las Vegas sounded exciting, so we went there. We had a fabulous time with each other and with the Lord. However, a few months later, I received a phone call from one of my associate pastors. It seemed that I was being mentioned in a sermon by an evangelist who was conducting a revival meeting in a town several hundred miles away. The evangelist, while preaching on holiness and repentance, said, "The pastor of the largest Charismatic church in Huntsville, Alabama, goes to Las Vegas to gamble and get drunk."

I was shocked. I was being used in a sermon as an example of a sinful Christian and preacher. I did not know how this was possible. I eventually discovered that when we innocently told one of my wife's relatives that we were going to Las Vegas for our anniversary and second honeymoon, we did not measure up to that individual's standard of holiness, and this relative told another preacher who told the evangelist who used me as an example of a sinner. The evangelist who said I was such a terrible sinner had never met me. He did not know me and had never even spoken to me. He certainly did not know my heart or my motives, and he did not have the actual facts. While presuming to preach on holiness, he was actually gossiping, slandering, and telling an entire church that I was an unholy preacher!

Many people preach their own personal, private convictions in the name of holiness and repentance as though these convictions were the Word of God. As a result, they judge others who do not agree with their personal convictions or live according to their standards. When other believers do not measure up, they are immediately judged, condemned, and held up before the Church as believers who are living in sin. Preachers have "slaughtered" many innocent people in the name of holiness. However, this judgmentalism is in itself a terrible sin that has destroyed many lives. It is a tragic paradox that some people who preach repentance and holiness are at the same time falling into the sin of judgmentalism as they preach that the rest of us are unholy.

Another passage that helps us understand what the Scriptures mean by "him whose faith is weak" is found in First Corinthians 8. In the days and culture of the early Church, eating meat that had been sacrificed to an idol was a disputable matter. Therefore there are a number of references in the New Testament that address this issue. First Corinthians 8 is one such passage. In First Corinthians 8:7 Paul says, "...Some people are still so accustomed to idols that when they eat such food they think of it as having been scarified to an idol, and since their conscience is weak, it is defiled." Romans 14 talks about a person's faith being weak, and First Corinthians 8 talks about a person's conscience being weak. In other words, there are believers who have a very sensitive conscience, so sensitive that they view many things in this life as sin.

In the area of disputable matters, there is nothing wrong with having a supersensitive faith and conscience, as long as you don't impose your faith and conscience on everyone else. Your personal faith and conscience are not the measures by which other people are to be judged. In the gray area of disputable matters, you are certainly entitled to your opinion. But your opinion is your opinion and not the Word of God on a particular issue. Private opinions must not be presented as the all-inclusive will of God for every single believer in the Body of Christ. People who strongly present their opinion as though it was the Word of God are in danger of controlling and manipulating people. Such control and manipulation is witchcraft.

Those of us who preach the Word of God must always be careful that we preach the true Word of God and not simply try to get people to do what we want them to do. Preachers move people, challenge people, inspire people, instruct people, warn people, and call people to obedience. But when we do so on the basis of our own opinion instead of the Word of God, we are in trouble and headed toward control and manipulation. I am not God, and my opinion is not divinely inspired! My opinion is good for me, but it may not be good for you.

Christ, Not Condemnation

Colossians clearly states, "So don't let anyone condemn you for what you eat or drink, or for *not* celebrating certain holy days or new-moon ceremonies or Sabbaths. For these rules were only shadows of the real thing, Christ himself. Don't let anyone condemn you by insisting on self denial..." (Col. 2:16-18 NLT). Why preach the shadow when the real thing has come? Those who preach rules are not preaching Christ. Rules were good until Christ came, but now Christ must be preached or we bring the people of God back under the law and its curse (see Gal. 3:10-11). The preaching of Christ is not the preaching of rules and man's opinions of what is right and what is wrong.

How sad it is that we are still hanging around the shadow and not Christ Himself. Even sadder is the fact that people respond to the preaching of rules more than they respond to the preaching of Christ. An erroneous, religious, self-righteous sermon on why a Christian should not drink wine or go to the movies gets more people to the altar than the preaching of Jesus Christ and the old rugged cross. I suggest that we quit preaching our own standards and get back to preaching Christ. Let's major on majors instead of majoring on minors. Christ is the major theme that we are to proclaim. And man's personal opinion of whether a Christian can buy a lottery ticket without sinning doesn't even qualify as a minor.

The Bible is clear that we are to accept our brothers and sisters without passing judgment on disputable matters. It is a sin to judge someone on the basis of your own convictions. We are not to "look down" on others who have a different level of faith and conscience, and we are not to "condemn" them (see Rom. 14:1-3). When we judge, look down on, or condemn others, we sin. The Bible is very explicit on this matter. Judgmentalism is named in the Bible, and we have both chapter and verse to show that it is never acceptable to God.

Not one of us is called to a "ministry of condemnation." The Lord Jesus had the opportunity to condemn a woman who had been caught in the very act of adultery. This woman had not transgressed in some disputable matter. She *had sinned*, and there was no doubt about it. Yet Jesus beheld her and said, "...neither do I condemn you..." (Jn.

8:11). How wonderful and kind Jesus is! He is not a condemner, and neither is the Holy Spirit. If a person is preaching on holiness and he is bringing heavy condemnation upon his listeners, along with a lot of his own personal or denominational opinions on disputable matters, realize that he is not operating by the Spirit of Jesus Christ. Even when presenting God's absolutes of right and wrong, Jesus was not a condemner of mankind. Condemnation belongs to the unbeliever, not the believer.

For God so loved the world that he gave his one and only Son, that whoever believes in him shall not perish but have eternal life. For God did not send his Son into the world to condemn the world, but to save the world through him. Whoever believes in him is not condemned, but whoever does not believe stands condemned already because he has not believed in the name of God's one and only Son (John 3:16-18).

I'm sad to have to say this, but the truth is that the most condemning people on the earth are religious people. Religion condemns and rejects people. Christianity should not be a religion. Jesus did not come to form a new religion. He came to save, heal, forgive, and bless broken, sinful humanity. When holiness is taken to an extreme, it always leads to judgmentalism and the rejection of brothers and sisters who do not live the way that *we think* they should live.

The man who eats everything must not look down on him who does not, and the man who does not eat everything must not condemn the man who does, for God has accepted him (Romans 14:3).

God accepts people whom the religious throw away. God accepts people whom others judge, condemn, and look down on. What if you went to the movies to watch *Schindler's List*? *Schindler's List* was an "R"-rated movie. There are some in the Body of Christ who would use you as a public example of an unholy Christian if they ever heard that you had watched an "R"-rated movie. This is because some people and some denominations have created a brand-new commandment, "Thou shalt not watch an 'R'-rated movie." Where did they get that commandment? They made it up. And they expect you to live by it and measure up to it. If you don't, they will label you as unholy. Of course, their condemning you for watching *Schindler's List* would also be a sin, but they won't see it that way.

I agree that there is a ton of garbage on television and in many movies, and many "R"-rated movies are filth. But there is no law of God that says you *can't* ever go to the movies or watch TV. The Holy Spirit will be your guide, and if you are watching something that He doesn't want you to watch, you will feel Him speaking to you and urging you inside. Yet the Bible has not given us any specific commandment that we can preach or hold over anyone's head regarding this issue.

Cultural Issues and Conviction

Romans 14 mentions the following three disputable matters: eating meat sacrificed to an idol; the day of the week we should worship God; and drinking wine. The first issue, eating meat sacrificed to an idol, is not an issue in our day or culture. Which day of the week we are to use for worship is still an issue with some, but not many, in our society. Drinking wine is still a disputable matter in the churches of America to this day. From this, I believe we can safely determine that many disputable matters are cultural in nature.

In America, drinking a beer is strictly taboo for a Christian. In Germany it is absolutely normal and acceptable for Christians to drink beer. Are the German brethren in sin? Are we American Christians more holy because of our strong stand that a born-again Christian should never drink a beer? Who is right and who is wrong? Is it a sin for a Christian to drink a beer or a glass of wine or is it not? This is a true disputable matter in our day and culture. Those who preach their own personal standard of holiness would say that it is undoubtedly a sin for a believer to ever drink wine or have a beer. But where is that commandment in the Bible? That commandment is not in the Bible, but it is in some denominational handbooks. Many who preach holiness and repentance are not preaching the Word of God. They are preaching the word of their denomination or their own personal belief.

I am declaring this to be a disputable matter even though I am personally a non-drinker. I certainly do not want to push anyone into true sin—and drunkenness and addiction are sins. I recognize that some people have addictive personalities. They cannot take a sip of wine without becoming hooked on it. Alcoholism is a terrible evil, and it is responsible for ruining many, many marriages and many children's lives. Alcoholism is incredibly destructive, and we have many chapters and verses in the Bible to show that drunkenness is a definite sin. But the issue of a single beer or glass of wine is not the same as that of drunkenness. If your doctor prescribed it for your health, would it still be a sin?

The answer to that question is up to you and your conscience. For some it is a sin. For others it is not.

Paul tells us that what someone believes about these things should be kept between that individual and God. If it is not a sin for you to have a glass of wine, that is fine, but keep it between yourself and God. If it is not a sin for you to watch television or go to the movies, keep it between yourself and God. In the area of disputable matters, what is acceptable for you may be a sin for someone else in the Body of Christ and may hurt his relationship with Christ.

One thing that we must be very careful about in this area of disputable matters is that Scripture instructs us that it is a sin to do anything that would cause our Christian brothers to fall (see Rom. 14:13). That's why Paul says that we are to keep things between ourselves and God. We don't want to eat meat, drink wine, go to the movies, or do anything else if it is going to cause someone with a weak conscience and faith to fall away from Christ. There are things that you can handle that will not cause you to fall away from Christ but may cause someone else to fall away.

We need wisdom and understanding here. Each of us is so different. We all have weaknesses, but not the same weaknesses. If you shut me up in a room with ten of the best bottles of wine money could buy, I would not be tempted in the least. I hate the taste of the stuff. The same holds true for beer or any kind of alcohol. But for someone else, such a temptation could prove to be his downfall. There are things we can encounter that can so negatively impact a person that he or she will fall away from God and turn to sin. Remember, what is not a temptation and allurement for you, can be so for someone else, and what doesn't bother someone else may be your greatest weakness.

Romans 14 is especially pertinent for these times. This chapter teaches us to accept our brothers and sisters in Christ and not reject those who have convictions different from our own. It shows us that personal convictions of conscience and private opinions must not be preached, *period*, much less preached as the Word of God. No preacher has the right or the authority to say that it is unrighteous or unholy for a Christian to go to the movies, go to the beach, drink a glass of wine, or make any other definitive ruling on a disputable matter. We are not to measure others by our convictions. We are to understand that there are some things that are sinful for one person but not sinful for someone else. And in all things we are to be considerate of our brothers and sisters and their consciences, and seek to do nothing that would lead someone else into what may be sin for him or her.

The Sin of Judgmentalism

We should not judge people on issues that are not clearly spoken of in the Word of God, nor should we judge people based on our own interpretations of circumstances and appearances. Have you ever noticed that we have the nasty habit of assuming the worst about people? We assume people are guilty rather than assuming they are innocent. This is something I am working to correct in my own life.

Such presumption and judgmentalism is sin. I recognized that it was still operating in my life one evening when my wife and I, along with two close friends, went for dinner at a local steak house. The restaurant was crowded, and there was a waiting line. While we were waiting for our table, I happened to notice that my family physician and her husband walked by and took a seat at the bar. Although I say that I am not religious, I still have some religion and judgmentalism that has not yet been fully rooted out, because when they took a seat at the bar I immediately judged them in my heart. I thought, *Oh my goodness, that's my doctor and she's at the bar drinking.* (Notice how I had immediately connected sitting at the bar with sin.) The truth is, I did see them walk by, and I did see them take a seat at the bar, but I did not see them drinking. But what if I had? I have already stated that I do not believe a single drink is necessarily a sin. However, in a split second, I had assumed my doctor was committing some sin. She was not. The sin was within me.

When we see someone in what we think is a sin, we rarely stop to consider any other point of view. In the example I just gave, perhaps my doctor had just finished a long, hard day at the office and did not feel like standing up while she was waiting for a table. Maybe she decided to take the only seat available in the crowded restaurant, which was at the bar. Even if she had a drink, what concern is it of mine? It's none of my business.

When my wife and I went to Las Vegas, my wife's relative and two preachers assumed that I was involved in some sin. They weren't there. They don't know what we did. Yet they assumed my guilt and passed it on to others. This type of presumption, judgmentalism, and unmerciful slandering of our brothers and sisters in the Body of Christ must come to an end. And we must choose that the change will begin with us.

A dear pastor friend of mine took a church that was in deplorable condition. Not many men would have even considered taking this church, but my friend did. After he had been there for awhile, a new woman came into the church. She needed counseling, and this pastor gave her loving pastoral care. After awhile, the woman began telling other church members that she was having an affair with the pastor. Soon the rumor spread all through the church, and the pastor was forced to resign. After he had left in total disgrace, the woman spoke up, "Oh yes, there is something I need to tell you all. I lied. The pastor and I never had an affair." This good man's ministry and reputation had been ruined, not because he sinned, but because he had been accused of sin and others assumed his guilt.

Accusation is one of satan's big guns. When he really wants to knock you down, he will bring some accusation against you, knowing that the accusation alone will be enough to overthrow you. Accusation works so effectively because people will automatically assume a person's guilt, rather than his or her innocence. Just let the accusation arise that some preacher is stealing money or is immoral and the accusation alone will often be enough to bring him or her down. Those who hear such an accusation also tend to cooperate more with the devil than with God. Too often we take delight at joining satan's team and begin to prosecute the accused without even knowing the truth or any of the facts.

I've noticed that whenever we hear of a crime on television or radio or when we read of crime in the newspaper, we assume that the person apprehended is guilty. Even though we are not on the inside of the case investigation and we do not know anything about it, we will still assume someone's guilt and sentence him in our hearts. How quick we are to judge others. Since the name *satan* literally means adversary and accuser, you would think that we would make ourselves less susceptible to his methods of attack.

Even when we are called upon to form an opinion about a matter, we need to remember that there are always two sides to every argument and issue. When you listen to one person, he or she will always seem right until another person comes along and gives a different perspective (see Prov. 18:17). However, most of the time we do not wait for both points of view. We take one point of view and use it to form our judgment or opinion. A truthful opinion cannot be formed until one hears both sides of a case.

A lot of judgmentalism would be stopped if we would just learn to mind our own business. People today are busybodies. Paul spoke about busybodies. He said,

We hear that some among you are idle. They are not busy; they are busybodies (2 Thessalonians 3:11).

Besides, they get into the habit of being idle and going about from house to house. And not only do they become idlers, but also gossips and busybodies, saying things they ought not to (1 Timothy 5:13).

People need to learn to mind their own business. Other people and their actions are not our business. We need to be concerned about ourselves and stop prying into other people's lives. Don't snoop around for sin in someone else's life. Get the log out of your eye, and then you will see clearly to get the speck out of your brother's eye (see Mt. 7:3-5). Often those who cry out the loudest about holiness are the ones who need it the most.

After Jesus' resurrection, Peter was worried about John and said, "Lord, what about him?" Jesus answered, "If I want him to remain alive until I return, what is that to you?" (see Jn. 21:21-23) In other words Jesus said, "Peter, be concerned about yourself. What I do with John is none of your business."

The root of judgmentalism is often found in the prideful rules of men. Again and again, people have violated the principle Paul established in Romans of keeping disputable issues between God and themselves as a matter of conscience. In Matthew 15:9, Jesus describes such people when He says, "They worship me in vain; their teachings are but rules taught by men." The King James Version puts it this way, "But in vain they do worship Me, teaching for doctrines the commandments of men." That last statement is a classic: "teaching for doctrines the commandments of men." That is exactly what is happening today. When we preach our own rules or our denomination's rules, as though they were God's rules, we bring people into all kinds of legalism and condemnation. This leads us to judge and reject other brethren who do not live according to our rules or our denomination's rules. Christ should be the basis of our fellowship with one another, not a body of rules. It is Christ and His work on the cross that should join us to our brothers and sisters in the Body, not in our doctrine about jewelry, hair length, drinking wine, or going to movies.

The Pharisees were devout religious leaders who were great at making up rules and using them to burden the people. In fact, they added their rules to God's rules. They expanded God's basic guidelines for living that He provided in the Ten Commandments into many hundred "Thou shalt nots." Then they changed God's rules to complement and support their man-made rules.

God's News Is Good News

Jesus rebuked the Pharisees for their hypocrisy and man-made rules. Jesus knew that the Pharisees had made life unbearable for God's people. Beware of any preacher who preaches a bunch of rules. We are to proclaim the *good news* of Jesus Christ, not laws, rules, and legalism. Are we preaching the gospel or are we preaching rules? If you hear an evangelistic message and there is no good news, then the gospel has not been preached.

I know of a young evangelist who was holding a series of meetings in a church. He preached on repentance every night, and every night the altars were filled. However, the pastor noticed that the people at the altar were the same people "repenting" over and over again, night after night. To some people, revival means getting people down to the altar in any way that you can. Going to the altar is fine, but is the Holy Spirit pulling you or is condemnation driving you?

I sincerely believe that I could get 90 percent of my Sunday morning congregation down to the altar every week if I wanted to. All I would need to do is preach against television, going to movies, listening to non-Christian music, smoking, drinking, etc. (And I must confess that it would probably do some of us some good.) I could preach a bunch of my personal convictions and rules, make people feel bad, and they would come. But are they coming to Christ? Are they coming to His blood? Are they coming by the Spirit? Or are they coming because I made them feel bad by manipulating them and beating on them with my personal standards of conduct?

Having said all this, I do believe that it is right to preach about sin, to preach God's standard, and then preach the good news. I am not against preaching God's standard. I am merely against anyone preaching his own rules as the standard.

Let's take our own personal, private judgments off of people. We are not God. Let's quit assuming that people are guilty when we honestly don't know. If I don't have the facts, I would rather err on the side of assuming innocence than assuming guilt. I would rather be too merciful, than too judgmental and hard on people.

When Ezra found out that there was sin among the Israelites, he and the other leaders set out to investigate the matter to ascertain the truth of who was guilty and who was not (see Ezra 10:16). If you have heard some type of gossip or remark accusing someone of a sin, at least have the integrity about yourself to investigate the matter before you form a negative opinion. Don't spread the rumor. Talk to the person who has been accused. Get his or her side of the story. Make a concerted effort to know all the facts and not just some of them. Get to the bottom of things before you form a judgment. That is the right way to go about it.

The Heart of the Matter

When forming judgments, we must not forget that there is a realm to a person that we cannot see and have no knowledge of. That realm is the realm of the heart and its motives. We can see a person's actions and hear his words, but we can't see his motives. If we understood a person's motives, perhaps we would be kinder and more gentle with him.

First Samuel 16:7 teaches us a great lesson with regard to appearances and their actual value to God and man.

But the Lord said to Samuel, "Do not consider his appearance or his height, for I have rejected him. The Lord does not look at the things man looks at. Man looks at the outward appearance, but the Lord looks at the heart" (1 Samuel 16:7).

Samuel was trying to identify the new king of Israel. He was just about to anoint Eliab, one of David's older brothers, when God stopped him. Samuel had fallen into the trap that we all fall into and that is of looking at the outside of man and not the inside of man. Eliab was so tall and handsome that Samuel jumped to the conclusion that Eliab must surely be the chosen one of God. As humans, we are all easily taken in by someone's outward appearance. We are not likely to consider a person's heart. That's why we make erroneous judgments. We're always looking at the outside of man. We are easily captured by a person's beauty, build, or accent. We're interested in the color of their eyes, hair, and skin. These things are the mere surface of a person. The real person is their heart.

The Lord looks at people differently than we do. God looks at the heart, thoughts, attitudes, and motives. God sees the real person. When a person is involved in sinful behavior, we look only at the behavior, but God looks at the person's heart. God sees things that we don't see. He understands things about a person that we don't understand. He is much more kind, tolerant, patient, and loving than we are. Maybe when we see someone in a sin we should not only disapprove of the sin, but we should try to understand the person and his heart and motives.

As a pastor I know that children who come from a divorced home are oftentimes wild and rebellious, despite the fact that their parents love them. Many parents struggle with the child or young person and can't understand how he could turn out this way. But I understand. That child or young person is hurt and angry. He is seething with anger over losing a God-given right and privilege of being part of a loving family where both parents are present. As time goes by, these kids strike out at their parents. On the surface friends, family, and teachers see rebellion and disobedience. But what about the children's heart? What's going on there? The answer is, they are angry. Anger and hurt are driving them to rebellion and disobedience. So the real problem is not rebellion and disobedience, but hurt, disappointment, and anger over not having both parents. You can minister more correctly to a person when God allows you to see the true inner man.

If we would only take the time to understand a person's heart and motives, how much more merciful we would be. If we saw a person's motives, we would not be so quick to assume guilt and render a harsh judgment. We would become more compassionate and loving to one another. We would fulfill the principles of Scripture, for we would bear each other's burdens in a useful, helpful way, and we would begin to experience unity among the Body of Christ.

Let's be kind, compassionate, and understanding. God is!

Chapter 5

True Repentance

When John the Baptist stepped out on the human scene, his message was "Repent!" When Jesus began His ministry, His message was "Repent." Obviously, *repentance* is a good, solid, biblical word. But what does it really mean?

As we study this topic, let me say right here and now that there is a difference between true biblical repentance and religious repentance. To many people brought up in churches that stress outward holiness, repentance refers to a call to sinless perfection. This is not biblical repentance.

A Work of God or Man?

When Jesus said, "Repent," was He telling us to get rid of all the sin and human frailties in our lives? No! First of all, if you or I had the ability to get rid of all our sin on our own, we would not need Him or His sanctifying work. If we had the power to perfect ourselves, Jesus wouldn't have had to die nor would He have needed to send the Holy Spirit to teach and guide us. He could have given us the command to become sinless and then let us work on it ourselves until we had accomplished perfection. Then, after we had accomplished it, He could have given us salvation. However, if we could perfect ourselves we would not need salvation. Salvation is for people who cannot save themselves. It is for people who sin and need a Savior. I am one of those people.

Humanism teaches that man can save himself. The Bible teaches that man cannot. You cannot get all the sin out of your life, and you will never be completely perfect in this life. Those who strain for personal perfection are living under a curse because they are trying to fulfill the law.

> *All who rely on observing the law are under a curse, for it is written: "Cursed is everyone who does not continue to do everything written in the Book of the Law." Clearly no one is justified before God by the law, because, "The righteous will live by faith." The law is not based on faith; on the contrary, "The man who does these things will live by them." Christ redeemed us from the curse of the law by becoming a curse for us, for it is written: "Cursed is everyone who is hung on a tree." He redeemed us in order that the blessing given to Abraham might come to the Gentiles through Christ Jesus, so that by faith we might receive the promise of the Spirit* (Galatians 3:10-14).

Earlier in the same chapter Paul had said, "You foolish Galatians! Who has bewitched you?...Did you receive the Spirit by observing the law, or by believing what you heard?

Are you so foolish? After beginning with the Spirit, are you now trying to attain your goal by human effort?" (Gal. 3:1-3) The King James Version translates the latter part of verse 3 this way, "...are ye now made perfect by the flesh?"

From the earliest generations of Christianity to the present, there have always been those who have tried to make themselves perfect and earn their salvation. I have been to Europe and have seen some of the old monasteries. I have also studied texts on other ancient monasteries that date back to the first, second, or third centuries after Christ. It was in these monasteries that men would renounce the world and take upon themselves vows of poverty and of silence as part of a human effort to become sinlessly perfect and holy. However, merely human efforts do not work and will inevitably fail to get the sin out of an individual. As we discussed in Chapter 2, what we need is the transforming of our hearts by the work of Christ and the transforming of our minds by the work of the Spirit and the Word.

Outward disciplines of the flesh cannot change the condition of the heart. As Paul wrote to the Colossians:

Such regulations indeed have an appearance of wisdom, with their self-imposed worship, their false humility and their harsh treatment of the body, but they lack any value in restraining sensual indulgence (Colossians 2:23).

Being sinlessly perfect may sound like a noble aspiration, but it always produces a life of condemnation and failure. If sinless perfection was possible, it would not come by discipline or human effort. Rather, it would come by the Holy Spirit working out the grace of God within us.

Become Mature

In your own struggle with the idea of perfection, you may have wondered about the verse that says, "Be perfect, therefore, as your heavenly Father is perfect" (Mt. 5:48). A person could read that verse, take it at face value, and strike out on a life of works, asceticism, and endless striving to become completely perfect. However, that person would only end up with a life of frustration and negative introspection. To find out what the word *perfect* in this verse really means you must look to the original Greek wording. The Greek word translated as "perfect" is *teleios*, which literally means, "completeness, of full age, man..." (James Strong, *Strong's Exhaustive Concordance of the Bible* [New York: Abingdon-Cokesbury Press, 1947], 71, #5046). Thus what the Bible means by "perfect" in this verse is completeness and full growth into maturity. Christian growth is a process, and we are to let that process continue and become complete in our lives (see also Phil. 1:6; Heb. 12:2).

I do not live under the false hope or illusion that I can be completely perfect and without sin in this life. It just won't happen! I do not live trying to make myself perfect, but neither do I use my inability to be sinless as an excuse to sin more (see Rom. 5:20–6:2). No, my friend, until the trumpet blows and the dead in Christ rise, you and I will have sin in our lives to deal with. We will need to resist sin and temptation every day of our lives.

In the Old Testament, the word *repent* (Hebrew, *shuwb*) literally means to turn back or to return (Strong's, #7725). Obviously the biblical meaning of the word *repent* is to turn away from the direction you are heading on your own and return to the Lord.

Turn Back to God

The first time "repent" is used in the Bible is in First Kings 8:46-49:

> *When they sin against you—for there is no one who does not sin—and you become angry with them and give them over to the enemy, who takes them captive to his own land, far away or near; and if they have a change of heart in the land where they are held captive, and repent and plead with you in the land of their conquerors and say, "We have sinned, we have done wrong, we have acted wickedly"; and if they turn back to you with all their heart and soul...and pray to you...then from heaven, your dwelling place, hear their prayer and their plea, and uphold their cause.*

In this passage, Solomon is praying about the future of the people of Israel. He is concerned that Israel might turn away from God. In his prayer he is basically petitioning God, "If they do turn away from You, O God, and if they do repent and turn back to You, please forgive them." Repentance means to turn back to God! It does not have anything to do with sinless perfection. It is a directional word. When you are headed away from God, you need to *repent*, or turn around, *and head back toward God.*

I repented in 1966. I had my whole life planned and was heading in my own direction. When Jesus revealed Himself to me, I turned around and turned toward Him. I left my own path and got on His path. I forsook my own will and hooked up to His will.

Jeremiah 15:19 says, "...If you repent, I will restore you...." The King James Version renders this phrase, "...If thou return, then will I bring thee again...." One translation uses the word *repent*; the other uses the word *return*. *Repent* and *return* are different translations of the same Hebrew word, which gives us additional proof that *repent* means "return."

In Isaiah 30:15 it is recorded, "...In repentance and rest is your salvation...." The King James Version translates this verse as, "...In returning and rest shall ye be saved...." Again repentance is shown to be a returning to God, not a state of sinless perfection.

Isaiah 59:20 uses the word *repent* this way: "'The Redeemer will come to Zion, to those in Jacob who repent of their sins,' declares the Lord." To repent of sin means to turn from it and turn to God. It is when we are in that posture that *God* can deal with our sin.

This is how we are to "repent" of sin in our lives. We are not to give in to sin or excuse it. As lovers of God, we must fight sin within ourselves and turn back to God when we do wrong. Be a person who is quick to confess your faults. You don't have to wail or weep to repent. If you do, that's fine. But you don't have to. When you sin, run to God and confess it boldly. Immediately declare to Him, "Father, I have sinned. I turn from it and I turn to You. Please forgive me and cleanse me with the blood of Jesus. In Jesus' name I ask this, amen." Learn to live in the truth of First John 1:9, which says, "If we confess our sins, he is faithful and just and will forgive us our sins and purify us from all unrighteousness." What a wonderful promise of mercy God has given us in this verse!

Embrace Faith

John the Baptist and Jesus both preached the message of repentance: "Repent, for the kingdom of heaven is near" (see Mt. 3:2; 4:17). The New Testament word for "repent" used here means "to think differently or...reconsider" (Strong's, #3340). (The call to repent is the call to change your mind and think differently about what you are doing and the direction you have been heading.) Mark 1:15 records Jesus' words as, "...Repent and believe the good news!" One of the biggest sins we are to turn from is the sin of unbelief. Jesus called people to turn from their unbelief and believe the gospel!

When John and Jesus stepped out on the stage of humanity, were they calling us to sinless perfection? No. They were preaching that mankind should change their mind for the better and reverse their direction. Consider Isaiah 53:6: "We all, like sheep, have gone astray, each of us has turned to his own way...." Because we each have turned to our own way, it was necessary for John and Jesus to arrive on the scene and say, "Hey, you need to change your mind and turn around. Turn from self and turn to God. Turn from the direction you're heading. You're heading away from God. Turn around and come to God."

One of Jesus' powerful statements about repentance is, "I have not come to call the righteous, but sinners to repentance" (Lk. 5:32). The Greek word here for "repentance" actually means "reversal." Sinners are to reverse their direction and their ways.

Many who preach repentance incorrectly say that once you truly repent, you will never commit that sin again. But Jesus said to the disciples, "So watch yourselves. If your brother sins, rebuke him, and if he repents, forgive him. If he sins against you seven times in a day, and seven times comes back to you and says, 'I repent,' forgive him" (Lk. 17:3-4). If Jesus instructed human beings to forgive and receive back again someone who continually transgressed against them, how much more is God able to do that since He is pure mercy, love, and grace?

There are people who sin and say, "I repent." When they say, "I repent," they sincerely mean it, but the flesh is weak and they fall into sin again. Are they not able to come back to God a second, third, fourth, or fifth time, if they need to? Certainly they can.

On the other hand, there are people who excuse sin and when they say, "I repent," they don't mean it. God knows our hearts and our sincerity in all things. Paul taught that we should repent and turn to God and prove our repentance by our deeds (see Acts 26:20). Although God will receive us when we sin and honestly repent, we should still sincerely endeavor to follow God's way rather than our own.

Repentance Requires Grace

God must give us the grace to truly repent. You and I cannot repent just out of decision and human volition. That is what happens every New Year's Eve. Many people create a list of New Year's resolutions—a list of all the things they intend to change about themselves in the new year. The list may look something like this: "I'm going to quit smoking.

I'm going to quit fussing. I'm going to quit drinking. I'm going to lose weight. I'm going to start exercising." Most of the time it only takes three weeks for these good intentions to falter. There is a vast difference between your trying to change yourself and God changing you.

Real repentance is when you turn to God and allow Him to change you. You and I have no power to actually change ourselves. That means we need God even more than we thought. He wants to change us. He can change us, and He will change us. If you walk with God and follow Him, one of the two of you is going to change, and it's definitely not going to be God. The Christian life is a life of constant growth, change, and development.

And we, who with unveiled faces all reflect the Lord's glory, are being transformed into His likeness with ever-increasing glory, which comes from the Lord, who is the Spirit (2 Corinthians 3:18).

Real, heartfelt repentance and life changes must therefore be given to us by God. When the Gentiles were brought into the Kingdom of God, the believers said, "...So then, God has granted even the Gentiles repentance unto life" (Acts 11:18). It is God who grants repentance! My friend, we are so depraved in and of ourselves that if God does not give us the grace to repent, we cannot do it. A lot of what the Church is calling repentance today is merely people exercising will power as a result of human emotionalism. However, sooner or later, will power will fail. Will power lets us down and disappoints us. When God grants you repentance, you will certainly have a part to play, but repentance is much more than a mere human decision to be good.

Ask God to give you repentance. Open your heart and life to Him. Be honest with God. But just because true repentance comes from God does not give anyone license to go right on in his or her sin and rebellion. The problem with preaching or teaching certain subjects is that there are always people who will wrongly apply the truth and use certain points of it as an excuse to remain in their sin.

No, my friend, set yourself against sin! You have no excuse to sin. Plead with God to plunge His holy scalpel into your heart and soul and operate on you and your sinful condition. Those who look for an excuse to sin prove that they are still in love with sin.

Turn around. Don't go your own way in life. Only God knows what is truly best for you. Trust Him. Get out of your car and into His car. Let Him drive. You may well say, "But I don't know where He'll take me." This is true, but neither did Abraham—and Abraham became the father of faith and of many nations. All I know is that God is good, and wherever He takes you will also be good. God never leads anyone down a wrong path. God has your best interest at heart. You can believe that. You may think that you know what is best for yourself, but you don't. Only God knows. Remember, "There is a way that seems right to a man, but in the end it leads to death" (Prov. 14:12).

Faith is trusting God as He takes control of your life. It is trusting that God is taking you somewhere good, somewhere better than you would have ever guided yourself to. It is by faith that you receive repentance and your salvation, and it is by faith that you will continue to walk in the goodness and grace of God.

Chapter 6

The Gift of Grace

Grace is an all-important New Testament word. Scripture often uses it in contrast to the idea of being under law: "...we are not under law but under grace..." (Rom. 6:15). With the giving of the Ten Commandments, the nation of Israel came under law as a means of obtaining right standing before God. Some might argue that faith was also involved in the law because the law officially instituted animal sacrifice, which required faith in the sacrifice to remove sin from an individual's life. I don't doubt that faith was involved to some degree in the Old Testament; but the major theme of the Old Testament is law, and the major theme of the New Testament is grace. Things have changed! The New Testament, which puts believers under grace, is a superior covenant with better promises and a superior sacrifice—the sacrifice of the Son of God!

Jesus—The Fulfillment of the Old Testament

Before the law, Abraham was made righteous by his faith. When the law was formally instituted, obeying the commandments of God became the basis of righteousness. As we read the New Testament, we find that there were people who still used obeying the commandments of God as a means to righteousness: "Zechariah and Elizabeth were righteous in God's eyes, careful to obey all of the Lord's commandments and regulations" (Lk. 1:6 NLT). Even Jesus was circumcised and lived according to the law: "Then it was time for the purification offering, as required by the law of Moses after the birth of a child..." (Lk. 2:22 NLT).

Many people are quite shocked to learn that Jesus was an Old Testament prophet. He was the last of the Old Testament prophets. The New Testament began with His death on the cross. That's why at the last supper Jesus said, "For this is My blood of the new testament, which is shed for many for the remission of sins" (Mt. 26:28 KJV). The blood of Jesus began the New Testament dispensation. His blood was the dividing line between law and grace. "For the law was given through Moses; grace and truth came through Jesus Christ" (Jn. 1:17).

Yes, the Lord Jesus was born under the law, or under the Old Testament. He lived His whole life under the law so that He might fulfill it and redeem each one of us: "But when the time had fully come, God sent his Son, born of a woman, born under law, to redeem those under law, that we might receive the full rights of sons" (Gal. 4:4-5). Jesus understood the day in which He lived, and He knew that He was the bridge from the old to the new. That's why after healing the man with leprosy, He said, "...But go, show yourself to the priest and offer the gift Moses commanded, as a testimony to them" (Mt. 8:4).

Jesus would not say that today! Why? Because He has already died for mankind, and with His death, burial, and resurrection, the New Testament was put into action. The New Testament is not a testament of law or works, but a testament of grace and love. The New Testament is not a testament of "Let's see what I can do to get God to love me and accept me." The New Testament is a testament of Jesus Christ and the truth that He has already done everything that can ever be done to make you righteous in God's sight. The Old Testament was, "What can I do?" The New Testament is, "What has Jesus done?" The Old is about you and your efforts. The New is about Jesus and His efforts. The Old is about working and earning righteousness. The New is about receiving the *free gift* of righteousness.

> *...how much more will those who receive God's abundant provision of grace and of the gift of righteousness reign in life through the one man, Jesus Christ* (Romans 5:17).

In each of our Bibles, there is a page inserted before the Gospel of Matthew that says, "The New Testament." Therefore, when we read Matthew chapter 1, we assume that we are reading the New Testament. But we're not! The New Testament doesn't start until Matthew 27:50, Mark 15:37, Luke 23:46, and John 19:30.

> *And when Jesus had cried out again in a loud voice, he gave up his spirit* (Matthew 27:50).

Jesus' death begins the New Testament. Everything that takes place before His death is Old Testament. Matthew says that when Jesus died, "At that moment the curtain of the temple was torn in two from top to bottom..." (Mt. 27:51). This is highly significant because it shows that Jesus' death opened the way for believing mankind to enter the very presence and glory of God. No longer did anyone need to obey the law to get into God's presence. The way into God's presence had been secured by the works of one man—Jesus Christ.

Free Access to God

As you can now see, the majority of the Gospels takes place under the Old Testament. The Book of Acts is the first real New Testament book of the Bible. And we find in this book a dispute among the followers of Jesus concerning the proper message of salvation. These men and women had lived all their lives under the law, and now a new, radical message was being preached. It was the message of salvation by grace through faith. Think of the changes these New Testament saints had to go through—the psychological and theological changes they wrestled with and were forced to accept. No longer was salvation received on the basis of merit or as a reward for good behavior or good works. It was a free gift to all who would believe. It was a free gift based on what someone else had done. Nothing was required other than to believe in Jesus as Lord and Savior.

There were some people who could not understand the message of God's grace and tried to bring the disciples back under the law. They could not grasp the concept that no one had to earn righteousness any longer. The idea was a complete shock to their system. They thought, *Surely, I have to do something.* But this was no longer true. Jesus had already done something that was sufficient for the righteousness of all, and salvation and righteousness became based on what He had done—period. Finally, a huge council was held in Jerusalem to discuss the problem of those who were trying to bring the New Testament saints back under the Old Testament law:

> *Some men came down from Judea to Antioch and were teaching the brothers: "Unless you are circumcised, according to the custom taught by Moses, you cannot be saved." ... Then some of the believers who belonged to the party of the Pharisees stood up and said, "The Gentiles must be circumcised and required to obey the law of Moses"* (Acts 15:1,5).

Avoid the Curse

There will be someone who does not understand righteousness by faith and will try to preach law, works, and human effort. Beware! Once you start enjoying life in Christ and the freedom that He has given you by grace, someone will try to bring you back into law and bondage. The devil wants you under law. He would prefer that you try to walk with God, by being good. Satan fights grace and the righteousness that comes by faith. He will use friends, denominations, preachers, and even misapplied Scriptures to try to drag you back into a legalistic religious system where you will be required to work hard to be good enough for God and Heaven. Satan knows that if he can keep you in bondage to laws and rules, then he has a legal right to curse you and your whole life.

*All who rely on observing the law are under a curse,
for it is written: "Cursed is everyone who does not
continue to do everything written in the Book of the
Law." Clearly no one is justified before God by the
law, because, "The righteous will live by faith." The
law is not based on faith; on the contrary, "The man
who does these things will live by them." Christ
redeemed us from the curse of the law by becoming a
curse for us, for it is written: "Cursed is everyone who
is hung on a tree." He redeemed us in order that the
blessing given to Abraham might come to the Gentiles
through Christ Jesus, so that by faith we might receive
the promise of the Spirit* (Galatians 3:10-14).

The word *cursed* means "doomed." People who try to be
good enough to merit God's love, acceptance, and forgiveness will only find themselves doomed, for they have
rejected God's righteousness and are trying to establish
their own. They are going against God's way of being righteous. Under the New Covenant, God has only one way to
be righteous and that is to put your whole faith and trust in
Jesus Christ and His work on the cross.

Isn't it ironic that a genuine Christian could be doomed
by trying to be "good"? There's nothing wrong with trying
to be good. We all need to be good people. But now that we
understand real New Testament righteousness, we are righteous, and therefore we choose to do good. However, we
don't do good to become righteous.

As we saw in Chapter 3, it is possible for a believer to
fall from grace. Falling from grace does not mean that you
lose your salvation. It means that your walk with God has
lapsed back into trying to be good enough or religious

enough to merit God's blessing. The apostle Paul addressed this issue in his Epistle to the Galatians:

> *You who are trying to be justified by law have been alienated from Christ; you have fallen away from grace. But by faith we eagerly await through the Spirit the righteousness for which we hope* (Galatians 5:4-5).

Many Christians today are in a state of being fallen from grace. The text does not say you have fallen away from God; it simply says that you have fallen from grace. You have begun to relate to God based on good works, human effort, and "doing the right things." After being saved by grace through faith, many people try to walk with God by effort, striving, and works. You are saved by grace through faith, and that is the basis of your whole relationship with God. You don't get saved by grace through faith and then institute a system of works through which you fellowship with God. You can't earn friendship with God. Friendship with God is a gift, given to those who trust Jesus. Friendship with God is available through grace to every believer. Intimacy with God only comes through Jesus Christ, and it is available right now to every born-again child of God.

> *Therefore, since we have been justified through faith, we have peace with God through our Lord Jesus Christ, through whom we have gained access by faith into this grace in which we now stand. And we rejoice in the hope of the glory of God* (Romans 5:1-2).

Through Jesus Christ we have gained *access* to God the Father. This access that we have been given, has been given to us because of faith and grace. "For through him we both have access to the Father by one Spirit" (Eph. 2:18).

Through Christ and by the Holy Spirit, we have access to the Father! You don't have access to the Father because you've prayed for ten hours. You don't get in to see the Father by putting in 20 hours of Bible study. Fasting 30 days will not give you access to the Father. Keeping the Ten Commandments doesn't do it either. No human being is so good and holy that his own goodness or holiness will get him to the Father's throne. Jesus' blood is the only thing that give us access into the presence of the Father.

Grace Can't Be Earned

Hopefully, you can now see that those who try to be good enough to win Jesus' favor are poor, misguided people. They may mean well, but they really don't believe or understand the old rugged cross or the blood of the Lamb. "Being good" and "religious works" are not substitutes for the cross and the blood. Salvation, righteousness, and even our daily fellowship with God is not based on grace *and* works. No! It is based entirely upon grace and faith—from beginning to end. Don't ever let anyone try to persuade you that the equation for salvation and righteousness is grace + faith + works + being good enough. That is an error of the gravest proportions.

Our contemporary churches have devised their own laws and list of works for a person to become righteous and have fellowship with God. There are Baptist laws, Methodist laws, Catholic laws, Presbyterian laws, Charismatic laws, Brethren laws, Pentecostal laws, and the list goes on. We have taken our personal standards of "right and wrong" and preached them as though they were the standard for every believer. Whoever does not keep our list of rules becomes condemned because we condemn them. Our rules and lists are just another way of burdening people with our personal requirements for righteousness and holiness. We declare that a certain behavior or activity is righteous or unrighteous, and we expect everyone to adhere to what we say. If they don't, not only are they "out," but we'll talk about them as they leave. This has nothing to do with God's gift of grace in righteousness, holiness, and salvation.

The nature of grace is summed up in Romans 11:5-6, "So too, at the present time there is a remnant chosen by grace. And if by grace, then it is no longer by works; if it were, grace would no longer be grace."

Earning and *deserving* are the very opposite of grace. Grace brings you things that you cannot earn and things you will never deserve. If you have earned something, then it can't be given to you by grace. Every week people go to work and earn a paycheck. That paycheck is not given to them by grace. It is not a gift. They deserve that paycheck. They have worked for it. They earned it.

We are working for and paying for our homes, cars, clothing, appliances, etc. After our home mortgage is paid off, we can say, "I worked for 30 years and paid for my house." We have earned that house. We deserve it because we have worked for it and paid for it ourselves. If, however, someone came up to you and gave you a house, absolutely free, then that house is a gift. It is given to you as a result of someone's good will toward you. You don't deserve the house. You didn't work for it. It was a free gift. That house came to you by grace, the unearned, undeserved, loving favor of an individual.

Let's say that someone bought you a birthday gift. It was a gorgeous piece of apparel, one you had been admiring for some time. It was presented to you by someone who loved you and felt good will toward you. That gift was given to you by grace. You didn't work for it, and therefore you did not deserve it. It was free, a gift of love! That is grace.

God works by grace. He loves us and gives us things that we did not work for and could never earn. He gives us the free gift of salvation, righteousness, holiness, and intimate friendship with Him. God looks favorably on us, looks kindly at us, and gives us many presents and gifts. I, for one, can never in all eternity pay Him back for these gifts. These gifts cost Him the life of His Son. The price paid to give me these presents is so great that it is beyond my ability to *ever* repay Him. I don't deserve His gifts and I have not worked for them. Indeed, they are so great that there is no work I could ever do to merit these gifts and presents. I just have to receive them and know that they are given to me by grace— a result of God's love and good will toward me.

Many people cannot enjoy the gifts of God in their lives because they are laboring to pay for them. Anything you do to pay God is called a "work." In Romans 11:6, the word used for "works" means toil. God's people are *toiling* to pay for their salvation, righteousness, and fellowship with God. Even those of us in full time ministry are sometimes fooled by satan into performing the duties of our ministries as an effort to "repay God" for all that He has given us. That's why so many people in the ministry are wearing themselves out, working harder and harder for bigger ministry. It is a result of believing the enemy's lie that the bigger our ministry becomes, the more we have "paid God back." Pastors are quitting the ministry at an alarming rate, and ministers are dropping dead of heart attacks all the time. Ministers are some of the most ambitious people on the earth, but if our ambition and ministry is just our "work" to pay Jesus back, then we too have fallen from grace!

Rest for the Weary

The heart-rending invitation Jesus gives in Matthew 11:28-30 applies to all who are working to earn God's blessings and to all who are working to repay God for His blessings. Jesus calls to each one, "Come to me, all you who are weary and burdened, and I will give you rest. Take my yoke upon you and learn from me, for I am gentle and humble in heart, and you will find rest for your souls. For my yoke is easy and my burden is light."

Jesus gives rest, not requirements. The load that He puts upon His followers is easy and light. He does not use a whip to drive anyone into a harsh, cruel, oppressive works program. It's not by works; it's by grace.

For it is by grace you have been saved, through faith—and this not from yourselves, it is the gift of God—not by works, so that no one can boast (Ephesians 2:8-9).

The council in Jerusalem summed up their meeting with this statement. "...We believe it is through the grace of our Lord Jesus that we are saved..." (Acts 15:11). In other words, salvation is a free gift! Enjoy the gift of His grace! That's what God wants you to do. Draw near to Him by His grace and experience the great joys of intimate relationship with Him.

Chapter 7

Life With the Spirit

We have examined the biblical concepts of salvation and righteousness by grace through Jesus Christ. We have seen that biblical holiness is at the same time an instantaneous gift, a continuing process, and a future promise. And we have briefly considered the role of the Holy Spirit in helping us to live for Christ in this world. Let's take some time to more closely examine the Holy Spirit's role in our Christian walk.

As we have seen, in the Old Testament God's people related to Him primarily through the law and the works of the law. In the New Testament, as we have seen, a person is saved by grace through faith as a result of the work of Jesus Christ. Yet to truly have a successful, intimate relationship with God, the believer must also come to know and respond to the work of the Holy Spirit in his or her life—the

Counselor (Comforter, KJV) that Jesus promised to send to teach and guide us.

The pages of the New Testament plainly show us that our lives revolve around the Holy Spirit and our fellowship and relationship with Him. As with the Father, our ability to have a relationship and close fellowship with the Holy Spirit exists only because of Jesus and His blood.

Relationship with the Holy Spirit now occupies the place once filled by the Old Testament law in the life of the believer. The Old Testament saints walked under the law. Today, because of Jesus, we walk with the Spirit. Please do not feel that by talking about the Holy Spirit, we are somehow pushing Jesus aside. Nothing could be further from the truth.

One of the things that Christians are ignorant of today is the different functions that the separate members of the Godhead perform. God the Father is our heavenly Father. But He sent Jesus—the Son—into the world to die on the cross and pay the price to bring every individual back to Himself. Jesus is Lord and Savior. Jesus is not the Father. God the Father occupies the role of heavenly Father. Jesus, who is God the Son, occupies the role of Savior. The Holy Spirit, who is also a member of the Godhead, occupies the role of Comforter and Companion. The Father sent the Son into the world. The Son sent the Spirit into the world (see Jn. 16:7).

Who Is the Holy Spirit?

When Jesus' redemptive work was completed, He went back to Heaven where He now sits at the right hand of the

Father. Shortly after Jesus went to Heaven, the Holy Spirit came down from Heaven (see Acts 2:1-4). He now fills the life of the believer and walks and talks with us. The Holy Spirit is personally present with each believer at all times, no matter where he or she may be.

Read and study the Gospel of John, chapters 14 to 16. You will be astounded at what Jesus said about the Holy Spirit. Here are just a few things Christ taught us in these chapters:

1. The Holy Spirit is sent by Jesus and the Father (Jn. 14:16; 15:26).

2. The Holy Spirit is called a *Counselor* or *Comforter* (Jn. 14:16). The word *Comforter* in the Greek means, "One called alongside to help" (W.E. Vine, Merril F. Unger, and William White, Jr., *Vine's Expository Dictionary of Old and New Testament Words* [Nashville: Thomas Nelson Publishers, 1990], 110-111). The Amplified Bible translates this Greek word as "Counselor, Helper, Intercessor, Advocate, Strengthener, and Standby." The Holy Spirit has been sent by Jesus and the Father to counsel us, help us, pray for us, strengthen us, and step in for us when we need Him to.

3. The Holy Spirit is going to be with us forever— throughout eternity (Jn. 14:16).

4. The Holy Spirit is the Spirit of truth (Jn. 14:17).

5. The world cannot accept the Holy Spirit, for it does not see or know Him (Jn. 14:17).

6. The believer is to know the Holy Spirit because the Holy Spirit will live with him and in him (Jn. 14:17).

7. The Holy Spirit comes to us in the name of Jesus (Jn. 14:26). That means that the Holy Spirit comes to us as Jesus' earthly substitute. He is here representing Jesus, filling Jesus' physical absence.

8. The Holy Spirit is to teach us "all things" (Jn. 14:26). When Jesus was here, He occupied the role of "Teacher." He was called "Rabbi" by His disciples. But now that He has left, another Teacher, the Holy Spirit, has been sent to replace Him and fill that role in the life of each of His followers. Jesus' teaching ministry continues in our day by the Person of the Holy Spirit.

9. The Holy Spirit testifies about Jesus (Jn. 15:26).

10. It was necessary for Jesus to go away in order for the Counselor to come to us (Jn. 16:7).

11. The Holy Spirit has a ministry of conviction to the world (Jn. 16:8-11).

12. The Holy Spirit guides us into all truth (Jn. 16:13).

13. The Holy Spirit does not speak on His own, but speaks only what He hears (Jn. 16:13).

(Many people believe that the Holy Spirit will never talk about Himself because the King James Version of John 16:13 says, "...for He shall not speak of Himself...." But the preposition "of" is better translated as "from." The Holy Spirit will not speak *from* Himself, as a source. Rather, the Holy Spirit repeats the words and teachings of Jesus. He hears from Jesus, and He repeats what Jesus is saying. The Holy Spirit will indeed speak of Himself if Jesus, the Head of the Church, wants to instruct a believer or His Body on the Person of the Holy Spirit. Indeed, the Holy Spirit is the member of the Godhead who authored the Holy Scriptures (see 2 Pet. 1:20-21), and in the Bible, the Holy Spirit is spoken of over 250 times. The Holy Spirit clearly speaks of Himself in the Bible and can give us instruction regarding Himself today.)

Jesus Christ: Our High Priest

The ministry of the Lord Jesus in our day is different from what we read in the Gospels. Although many believers do not understand this, we must view the New Testament as a progressive revelation of Jesus Christ. As the incarnate Christ, He came into this world and performed awesome deeds. But when He ascended into Heaven and sent the Spirit to take His place on the earth, we begin to see in Scripture a new dimension of the Lord Jesus. The Book of Hebrews reveals Him in a role far different than is shown in the Gospels. In Hebrews, Jesus is in the role of great High Priest. He is still Lord, Savior, Master, and Redeemer. But His present-day role is that of our great High Priest. Although Jesus does not change, His role has. He has given the tasks of His earthly ministry over to His Body to perform through the Holy Spirit (see 1 Jn. 4:17). And in His current position at the right hand of the Father, He serves as a heavenly priest and intercessor for us with the Father (see Rom. 8:34; 1 Tim. 2:5).

In Revelation, we are given yet another picture of Jesus. In Revelation, Jesus is the returning King who will conquer all His enemies and set up His Kingdom in Jerusalem. From His throne in Jerusalem, He will rule the world for 1,000 years. The Jesus you see in Revelation appears different from the Jesus portrayed in the Gospels or the Epistles. Why? His role has changed. Again, Jesus has not changed, but His role has. Our revelation of Jesus cannot stop with the Gospel of John; it must include the Scriptures as a whole and the things they have to show us about Him.

Because Jesus' role changed when He ceased to physically walk on this earth, He sent the Holy Spirit to live on this earth with His disciples. The Spirit, who is a real Person, continues the teaching ministry of Jesus, as well as His ministries of healing, miracles, and deliverance. Jesus' earthly ministry continues to this day. However, it continues through the Person of the Holy Spirit and through believers as we walk with God through the Spirit.

Now that we are under grace and living within the New Covenant, the law and its rules will always fail to make us right with God or bring us into closer relationship with Him. Rules are no longer the way to walk with God. They are not the way to relate to God. Ephesians makes it clear that the work of Jesus Christ has removed the validity of the law for the believer, "For he himself is our peace, who has made the two one and has destroyed the barrier, the dividing wall of hostility, by abolishing in his flesh the law with its commandments and regulations..." (Eph. 2:14-15). Colossians goes on to say, "...He forgave us all our sins, having canceled the written code, with its regulations, that was against us and that stood opposed to us; he took it away, nailing it to the cross" (Col. 2:13-14).

The Holy Spirit: Our Counselor and Guide

The law no longer stands between man and God. It was nailed to the cross. Therefore, we now relate to God through the Holy Spirit—who is God Himself. Our relationship with the Father is through Jesus and by the Spirit (see Eph. 2:18). If you have never met the Holy Spirit, your life with God will be greatly impeded. Mine was for 29 years. Since I met the Holy Spirit, everything in my life has improved dramatically—including my closeness to God.

May the grace of the Lord Jesus Christ, and the love of God, and the fellowship of the Holy Spirit be with you all (2 Corinthians 13:14).

Notice the phrase "the fellowship of the Holy Spirit." *Fellowship* means "partnership, participation, social intercourse, and communication." In modern English, we would say, "friendship." Friends talk to each other. Friends do things together. Friends are friends because they have regular social interchange. That is what we are to have with the Holy Spirit. He is to be the closest, most intimate, personal friend we have. We are supposed to talk to Him, and He is supposed to talk to us. This is all called "walking in the Spirit." Actually, we may better understand the concept if we refer to it as "walking *with* the Spirit."

Walking with the Spirit is a phrase that speaks of our close, intimate fellowship with the Person called the Holy Spirit. Our every day is to be spent in fellowship with the

Holy Spirit. Our whole Christian life is a life of walking with the Holy Spirit. The old hymn that says, "And he walks with me and he talks with me..." is true when you understand that it is the Holy Spirit who is walking with you and talking to you today. We may say, "What a friend I have in Jesus." But Jesus is not physically here at this time; He is in Heaven performing the ministry of the great High Priest. The Holy Spirit was sent here by Jesus to be your friend and ever-present companion. Therefore, I also say, "What a friend I have in the Holy Spirit!"

The Holy Spirit, while a different Person from Jesus and the Father, is also exactly like Jesus and the Father. He is so much like Jesus and the Father that He is called the Spirit of Jesus, the Spirit of Jesus Christ, the Spirit of Christ and the Spirit of God, the Spirit of the Father, and the Spirit of God (Acts 16:7; Phil. 1:19; Rom. 8:9; Mt. 10:20; Gen. 1:2, respectively).

We have tragically demoted the Holy Spirit today so that many see Him as little more than an angel. Some think He is some type of ambiguous mystical power that we are to get hold of. This is completely inaccurate. The Holy Spirit is a wonderful, living, eternal Person, and He has a specific role to play in the life of the believer today.

Some preachers think of the Holy Spirit as some type of impersonal power or anointing, rather than the real Person and member of the Holy Trinity that He is. Therefore, they believe it is almost heresy if someone admits to speaking to the Holy Spirit. The Holy Spirit is as much God as Jesus is. He is as much God as the Father is. The Holy Spirit is God! When you talk to the Holy Spirit you are talking to God. How tragic it is that there are preachers who will talk to their dog, cat, and canary, but still believe that it is sin to talk to God the Holy Spirit!

Intimacy With God Through the Spirit

Romans and Galatians, the two New Testament books that speak most clearly about our freedom from the law and the righteousness that comes to us by faith, are also the two books that provide the most insight regarding the Holy Spirit and His role in these New Testament times. Let's look at a few things these two books have to say about our relationship with the Holy Spirit.

But now, by dying to what once bound us, we have been released from the law so that we serve in the new way of the Spirit, and not in the old way of the written code (Romans 7:6).

We have been released from the law so that we can walk with God in a brand-new way, the way of the Spirit. Our relationship with God is no longer by law and works. That is the old way; the Scripture just quoted says so. Now we walk with God by the Spirit. That's hard to do if you don't know the Holy Spirit. You have to know Him and talk to Him to be able to live this Scripture. When people don't know the Holy Spirit, they are more likely to revert back to the law because of the big void in their spiritual life.

Not knowing the Holy Spirit and not being intimate friends with Him creates a huge empty place in your Christian life. People want to fill that empty place with something, so they try to fill it with good works and religious activity. In doing so, however, they fall from grace, come under law, and are doomed—cursed. Romans 7:6

above tells us that there is an old way and a new way of relating to God. Are you trying to make yourself "good enough" by keeping laws and rules, or are you walking in fellowship and closeness with the wonderful Holy Spirit? Are you relating to God the old way or the new way?

> *...through Christ Jesus the law of the Spirit of life set me free from the law of sin and death* (Romans 8:2).

The Holy Spirit is called "the Spirit of life." The Spirit gives life to a person. He brings life to an individual. The law, legalism, rules, and trying to be good enough only bring death. Simply put, walking in friendship with the Holy Spirit is life. Trying to obey a bunch of rules results in death. Which would you rather have, life or death?

> *For what the law was powerless to do in that it was weakened by the sinful nature, God did by sending his own Son in the likeness of sinful man to be a sin offering. And so he condemned sin in sinful man, in order that the righteous requirements of the law might be fully met in us, who do not live according to the sinful nature but according to the Spirit* (Romans 8:3-4).

What the law was powerless to do, God did! He did it by sending His own Son to be a sin offering. And in the sending of His Son to be a sin offering, the righteous requirements of the law were fully met in us! That means that because of Jesus, God looks at you as though you have fully kept the law and have never failed in even the smallest way. You can't keep the law! But because of what Jesus did on the cross, God looks at you as though you have kept it perfectly all your life! And this truth is *only* for those who walk with the Spirit and trust in Jesus' sacrifice on the cross.

As New Testament believers, we are to live according to the Holy Spirit, or in fellowship with the Holy Spirit. He has taken the place of the law. Our life revolves around Him. In the Old Testament, the individual's whole life was centered upon the law. The law was on that person's mind night and day. His daily goal was to continue to keep every jot and tittle. That is all over now. Jesus ended it. Now the Spirit is on our mind night and day, and our daily goal is to enjoy His sweet presence.

The mind of sinful man is death, but the mind controlled by the Spirit is life and peace (Romans 8:6).

We are supposed to be so close to the Holy Spirit that He even controls our minds and thoughts. Our minds are not to be filled with the keeping of rules and laws. We are not to be constantly scrutinizing ourselves for flaws. We are not to be working to become perfect in God's sight. Through the blood of Jesus we are already perfect in God's sight. Let's enjoy God. Jesus did the work that makes us perfect in God's sight. The only thing that we can do is believe on Jesus, and we can only believe on Jesus by an act of God's grace. Faith comes by grace. And the grace and faith that God gives allow us to receive and walk in the life and peace of the Spirit.

Holiness Through the Spirit

For if you live according to the sinful nature, you will die; but if by the Spirit you put to death the misdeeds of the body, you will live (Romans 8:13).

Close relationship with the Holy Spirit is the antidote to the poison of sin that lives within each of us. It is by the Spirit that we can kill the sin that lives in our bodies. Rules don't kill sin. Rules make us aware of sin's presence within us. Rules tell us what we shouldn't do. It is only by the Holy Spirit that we gain the power and motivation to truly be renewed in our minds and bodies and resist the temptations and sins that we encounter.

To further examine this point, we can say that people sin because of the pleasure it brings them. It is their only reason. Smoking, drinking, swearing, judging, sleeping around, and taking drugs all bring a certain kind of pleasure to a person. It is a fleeting pleasure and a deceptive pleasure, but it is a pleasure nevertheless. People don't want to give up their sin because they don't want to lose the pleasure.

Rules don't bring pleasure; they bring guilt and condemnation. Rules make us feel bad about ourselves. I'm not saying that there is never any place for rules, but rules don't cure us of sin. Rules don't bring pleasure, so people rarely give up their sin for rules. However, as strange as it may sound, legalism itself can bring a kind of pleasure to a person. Obeying a code of rules and laws makes a person feel good about himself. It makes a person feel that he has accomplished something. This is deceptive too, especially when talking about relating to God. If you feel good about yourself because you keep a code of ethics and a list of religious rules, you have fallen from grace.

Many people feel good about themselves because they keep the Ten Commandments. They obey religious law. That makes them feel as though they have earned something and deserve something. They even boast about "their righteousness." But the Bible says, "Let him who boasts boast in the Lord" (1 Cor. 1:31b). Doing good deeds or abstaining from bad deeds is nothing to boast about. We are to boast about Jesus, His love for us, and His death on the cross.

Since the sins of the flesh and the sins of the ego offer a fleeting pleasure, people keep returning to these sins to attempt to maintain their pleasure or self-satisfaction. For a person to abandon his sinful behavior, he must be offered a greater and more lasting pleasure and so switch pleasures. The Holy Spirit is the greater pleasure that God has for us! The Scripture says, "Taste and see that the Lord is good..." (Ps. 34:8). The presence of the Holy Spirit is an experience far better than any sin could ever hope to offer. To be in God's presence for ten seconds is a far greater pleasure than all the alcohol in the world could ever provide.

The psalmist knew the pleasure of the presence of God: "...in Thy presence is fulness of joy; at Thy right hand there are pleasures for evermore" (Ps. 16:11 KJV). Can you imagine fullness of joy? Fullness of joy is not found in a bar, cigarette, or drug. It is not found in adultery, homosexuality, or pornography. Fullness of joy is not found in obeying religious rules and laws. Keeping the commandments does not bring joy. Only the presence of God brings fullness of joy. His presence is a pleasure that is so great, so awesome, and so wonderful that people would gladly give up every other form of pleasure to get near Him if they only knew about it. It is the presence of God that we experience through a personal, intimate relationship with the Holy Spirit that changes our hearts and empowers us to stop sinning and willingly choose godly behavior.

...those who are led by the Spirit of God are sons of God (Romans 8:14).

In the New Testament, the Holy Spirit is our leader. We must be His followers. We are to allow the Holy Spirit to lead us in every situation in life. Again, it is difficult to be led by the Spirit if you don't know the Spirit. If you are unacquainted and unfamiliar with Him, you will not recognize His voice or be sensitive to His promptings.

Does God give you his Spirit and work miracles among you because you observe the law, or because you believe what you heard? (Galatians 3:5).

The Old Covenant was the law and the legalistic observances of rules and commandments. The New Covenant is a covenant of faith and the Spirit. Don't try to walk in the New Covenant in the old way. That's what many are doing today and their lives are filled with rigor rather than relationship. The Old Covenant was rigor and self-effort. The New Covenant is relationship by faith and grace.

So I say, live by the Spirit, and you will not gratify the desires of the sinful nature (Galatians 5:16)

"Live by the Spirit." The Greek word for "live" means "to follow as a companion" (Strong's, #4043). As we have discussed, we are gloriously invited to have a very close, personal relationship with the Holy Spirit. As we fellowship with Him and follow Him, we will find ourselves no longer desiring sinful things. Get over into the Spirit and you will not want anything the world or the flesh has to offer. The Amplified Bible says this about our relationship with the Holy Spirit,

However, I am telling you nothing but the truth when I say it is profitable (good, expedient, advantageous) for you that I go away. Because if I do not go away, the Comforter (Counselor, Helper, Advocate, Inter-cessor, Strengthener, Standby) will not come to you [into close fellowship with you]; but if I go away, I will send Him to you [to be in close fellowship with you] (John 16:7).

Jesus has sent the Holy Spirit to be in close fellowship with us. The closer we get to the Holy Spirit, the less appeal our bodily desires will hold for us.

But if you are led by the Spirit, you are not under law (Galatians 5:18).

Under the Old Covenant, people were led by the law. Today, we are led by the Holy Spirit because He now occupies the place once held by the law. Our whole life revolves around the Holy Spirit and not any individual's personal rules of righteousness and holiness.

Walk in Life

The verses that best sum up the difference between the Old Testament and the New Testament are found in Second Corinthians 3:6-11:

He has made us competent as ministers of a new covenant—not of the letter but of the Spirit; for the letter kills, but the Spirit gives life. Now if the ministry that brought death, which was engraved in letters on stone, came with glory, so that the Israelites could not look steadily at the face of Moses because of its glory, fading though it was, will not the ministry of the Spirit be even more glorious? If the ministry that condemns men is glorious, how much more glorious is the ministry that brings righteousness! For what was glorious has no glory now in comparison with the surpassing glory. And if what was fading away came with glory, how much greater is the glory of that which lasts!

This passage of Scripture calls the Old Testament "the letter"; "the ministry that brought death"; and "the ministry that condemns men." Do you really want to go back to earning God's love, approval, forgiveness, and blessings? Do you want to go back to death and condemnation? Do you want to go back to curses and doom?

Notice that the New Testament is called "the ministry of the Spirit" and "the ministry that brings righteousness." Compare the two. Death and condemnation versus the Spirit and righteousness. There is no comparison!

In that same chapter of Corinthians the Bible says, "Now the Lord is the Spirit, and where the Spirit of the Lord is, there is freedom" (2 Cor. 3:17). This is not a freedom to go out and live any way you want and to commit one sin after another. But it is a freedom from law, works, effort, rigor, and legalism as a means of attaining righteousness, holiness, and relationship with God.

My friend, enjoy your new relationship with God. Come to Jesus and let Him give you rest. Take up His yoke. Lay your heavy burden down. You are already righteous and holy in His sight through the blood of Jesus. Accept that by faith. Now enjoy the presence of the Lord that is given to you by grace, as a free gift. Let the Holy Spirit draw you closer to God and purify your heart and mind. It is time for you to stop striving and to rest in the relationship God has for you.

Chapter 8

Walking in Holiness

Does Grace Encourage Sin?

Why not say—as we are being slanderously reported as saying and as some claim that we say— "Let us do evil that good may result"? Their condemnation is deserved (Romans 3:8).

What then? Shall we sin because we are not under law but under grace? By no means! (Romans 6:15)

There is a danger in preaching the grace of God. There always has been. Even Paul realized the danger in making the transformation from law to grace. When Paul preached grace, he had to beware of two types of individuals. The first type of person was the Christian who felt that grace gave him a license to sin. The second type of person was the critic of grace, who would accuse Paul of encouraging the people to do anything that they wanted to do.

Today many people are steeped in what has been called "greasy grace." The person who holds to this belief will reason something like this: "I am under grace. God loves me no matter what I do. My deeds don't earn me any righteousness. It's not what I do that counts. It's what I believe, and I believe in Jesus. So I can go ahead and sin, if I want to. It won't matter. God will love and accept me regardless. So a little sin isn't going to hurt anybody. I'm under grace."

There are people like this today, just as there were in Paul's day. However, such people ignore some very real biblical principles about the consequences of our actions, particularly with regard to sin. The grace of God may give us freedom from law; however, it does not give us freedom from the consequences of sin. The truth is, you *can* sin, but you will pay for it—even under grace.

The Consequences of Sin

Whether an individual is under the Old Testament or the New, sin still comes with a high price tag. It is never free. Sin presents itself as though it is free, but in the end, it will always present the bill—and you will have to pay it. Even if you turn to God and trust the blood of Jesus as payment for your sin, you must still face the consequences of your sinful actions. All sin has consequences. Jesus paid the complete price for your forgiveness, righteousness, and salvation, but evil consequences will still present themselves to you as a result of the wrong actions you have chosen.

Let me give you a couple of examples. Let's say that you purposely started a forest fire. An entire forest was burned down and thousands of acres were ruined. Now, let's say that after you started the fire and saw the destruction it caused, you were conscience-stricken. You realized that you had done a horrible thing. You were greatly upset with yourself and finally called out to God and confessed that you burned down the forest. When you cried out to God, you were heartbroken and sincere. God heard you and graciously forgave you. You felt peace and release from guilt. Because of God's forgiveness you became righteous in God's sight again and entered into good standing with Him. But if you passed by the charred forest the next day, you would see that it was still burned down. The fact that God forgave you did not undo the deed and reverse what you had done. His forgiveness did not undo your arson.

What if you went to bed with a woman who was not your wife? Afterward, you felt horrible. You knew that you had sinned. You went home, and there was your wife. You had to look her in the eyes and act as if nothing was wrong. After a few days, you could not take it any longer. Terrible guilt was eating you up, so you knelt down, sobbing, crying out to God, and asking Him to forgive you for adultery. God is kind, loving, and gracious. He forgave you just like He said He would in First John 1:9. The heaviness lifted, and you instantly felt better. You rose to your feet determined that you would never fall into infidelity again. Things seemed to smooth out; everything was going fine. Weeks passed. Then one day the phone rang in your office. It was the other woman. She has just been to the doctor, and she is pregnant. Furthermore, she phoned your home this morning looking for you and your wife answered. They talked. Your wife knows. Misery closes in on you again, and sin has just presented you with the bill, the consequences of your sin. You think, *But I'm forgiven*. And yes, you are forgiven, and God remembers your sins no more. However, the woman is still pregnant, and your wife is still devastated. You have two huge messes to clean up.

When you arrive home you are scared and don't know what you will find. When you open the door, you see that your wife and her belongings are gone. All that is left is a note that says she is never coming back. You cannot blame God for your situation, for you are reaping the consequences of your own choices. You have messed up your own life. You destroyed your marriage. And now you must face up to it.

Let's say a month later your cellular phone bill comes in the mail. On it are billed all the calls you made to the other woman, including a number of long-distance calls. The bill for the one month is way over $800. Of course, you are out of that relationship now. God has forgiven you. But the phone bill is still due. The $800 must still be paid. God's forgiveness and grace did not cancel the bill you owe to the cellular phone company. Jesus paid for your sins, but you have to pay for your calls.

The Long Arms of Sin

Sin is no respecter of persons. There are repercussions to everyone's sins. Adam and Eve sinned and God forgave them. But their sin cost them the paradise they lived in and the sweet fellowship with God they enjoyed. Because Adam and Eve were our first parents, what they did affected all human beings. People are now born into this world with a fallen, sinful human nature. We are still dealing with the consequences of Adam and Eve's sin thousands of years later.

You see, no one sins alone. Our sins affect the people around us. Many times, it affects the ones we love the most. The alcoholic father does not only ruin his own life, but he also ruins the lives of his children. There is a price tag to being an alcoholic. And the unfair thing is that the alcoholic himself is rarely the only one who has to pay the bill for his sin. His innocent family members are stuck with the check as well.

Immorality ruins the lives of the two participants, as well as their relationship with their spouses and the lives of their children. Even if the two people are single, their sinful sexual exploits may very well destroy a wonderful future relationship. In addition, if you act immorally and contract a disease, you will most likely pass that disease along to someone you really love. No one sins alone. Our sins affect many, many other people, oftentimes innocent people who should not have to pay our bill.

You can mark it down: Your sin will hurt you, and it will hurt other people who love you, even while you are living under grace. Grace brings forgiveness, righteousness, and holiness, but it does not cancel the natural consequences of sin.

King David loved God. He fought Israel's enemies and won. He was the sweet psalmist of Israel and composed songs that would become Holy Scripture. God blessed him in every way. He was honored by God and man. Yet he sinned. He committed adultery, was responsible for the death of Uriah, lied, and covered up his sinful tracks.

Finally God sent Nathan the prophet to confront David with his secret sin. David fell down before Nathan. He confessed and repented of his sin. God spoke to Nathan and told him to tell David that he was forgiven and would not die, "but...." If only the word *but* had not been a part of God's message to David, everything in David's world would have returned to blessed prosperity. Nevertheless, there was a "but" to the message, and it was a message that David did not want to hear. He was forgiven, but the child Bathsheba had conceived would die and the sword would never leave David's house.

Shortly after Nathan delivered this message to David, the child that he and Bathsheba conceived did die. All hell broke loose in David's family, just like God told him it would. Amnon, a son of David, fell in love with Tamar, the daughter of David. Amnon raped Tamar and disgraced her. When Tamar's brother Absalom found out about it, he seethed with anger and bitterness, and over the course of time, he murdered Amnon.

As if that was not enough, Absalom undercut David with the people of Israel, turning the people away from his father. Absalom overthrew his father and took the throne of Israel away from David. David and his royal cabinet fled from Absalom and his followers, sneaking out through the darkness of night. David, the highly successful and respected king, was run off of the throne and out of town by his own son. The humiliation and shame were unbearable. Later, in a battle between David's forces and Absalom's forces, Absalom was killed. David wept, mourned, and lamented.

David brought all this misery on himself because of his sin. He was a man who was forgiven by God, but he ended up with two dead sons, a daughter who was raped, several of his wives raped by Absalom, and a temporary loss of the royal throne of Israel. All this was the result of a one-night stand with a beautiful woman whom he thought he had to have. What a price tag! The cost of David's escapade was far greater than he ever imagined. If only sin would present its price tag before it presented its temporal pleasure, we would be much more likely to resist. But there is a lie in every sin. The lie is that you will not get caught, and that there will not be any consequences to your actions.

David sinned again when he pridefully chose to count the number of warriors in his kingdom. This highly displeased the Lord, and God gave David the choice of three different consequences. The end result was that 70,000 innocent people in Israel lost their lives. David recognized the innocence of the people, and he cried out to God, "...I am the one who has sinned and done wrong. These are but sheep. What have they done? O Lord my God, let your hand fall upon me and my family, but do not let this plague remain on your people" (1 Chron. 21:17). Our sins have an impact on other people.

There are always, always consequences to sin. There was for Adam and Eve. There was for David. And there will be for you and me. Sin may look good. It may even look like the right thing to do. But sin is a lie, and it is out to trick you just like satan tricked Eve.

You Reap What You Sow — Sow Wisely

The Scriptures adamantly tell us that, even under grace, there are consequences to sin:

> *Do not be deceived: God cannot be mocked. A man reaps what he sows. The one who sows to please his sinful nature, from that nature will reap destruction; the one who sows to please the Spirit, from the Spirit will reap eternal life* (Galatians 6:7-8).

What you do will come back to you. If you do good, good will come your way. If you do bad, bad will come. The deeds you do are seeds that you plant. If you commit adultery, then you have planted a bad seed in the ground that will grow and sprout its own fruit. When God graciously forgives you, He does not pull the seed that you planted out of the ground. He allows it to remain, grow, and bear fruit. God has set forth the principle that a man reaps what he sows. If you don't want a tree to grow, then don't plant the seed. That's the only way to keep the tree from growing. If you don't want to harvest a bad crop, don't plant bad seeds. If you want to harvest a good crop, plant good seeds. What you get is what you plant. The difference in the fruit is in the seed!

There are many Christians today who kneel at the altars of their churches weekly, seeking help for the situations that they find themselves in. However, many of the situations we have in our lives have been produced by the seeds we have planted by our choices and actions. We are reaping the consequences of our past actions in our current circumstances. Consequences are for our good! When we come to understand how they work, they can keep us from doing wrong. Consequences will put the fear of God in an individual. We can't ever sin and expect to just get away with it.

Nothing Stays Secret

...and be sure your sin will find you out (Numbers 32:23 KJV).

This verse means that you can count on the fact that your hidden sin will not stay hidden. It will be exposed. People think that they can sin in private and get away with it. That is one of the deceptions of sin. For God sees everything, everywhere. There is no such thing as "private" when you realize that the eyes of the Lord are everywhere beholding everyone. Also, it doesn't matter where you sin or who on earth knows about it, it is still a seed planted that will come up against you. And you will feel the effects of sin in your own soul—whether you sin alone or in front of 500 people. Sin will come to light. It may take years for that to happen, but your sin will find you.

The Hebrew word for "find" in Numbers 32:23 literally means, "to come forth or to appear" (Strong's, #4672). Sin has a way of appearing here on earth, even after a person is forgiven and God has forgotten about it. It's part of reaping what you sow. If you don't want something embarrassing to suddenly one day appear, then don't plant the seed, even in secret. Secret seeds come up too. God is not ever going to be mocked.

This principle works not only on the deeds we do but also on the words that we speak. How many times have you said something to someone even in private, only to have your words thrown back in your face by the very person you were hiding them from? Words have a way of traveling. Most of us have learned that. Words are seeds too. Plant words of gossip, slander, criticism, and judgmentalism, and that is what you will reap in your own life.

For out of the abundance of the heart the mouth speaketh. A good man out of the good treasure of the heart bringeth forth good things: and an evil man out of the evil treasure bringeth forth evil things. But I say unto you, That every idle word that men shall speak, they shall give account thereof in the day of judgment. For by thy words thou shalt be justified, and by thy words thou shalt be condemned (Matthew 12:34b-37 KJV).

We reap what we sow, forgiveness notwithstanding. If there is anything that we have been duped into believing in our era of erroneous teachings on grace, it is the thinking that if we will simply confess our sins and claim God's forgiveness, then all the consequences of what we have done will be quickly whisked away. However, as Charles Swindoll points out in his excellent book, *David, A Man of Passion & Destiny*:

"Grace means that God, in forgiving you, does not kill you. Grace means that God, in forgiving you, gives you the strength to endure the consequences. Grace frees us so that we can obey our Lord. It does not mean sin's consequences are automatically removed. If I sin and in the process of sinning break my arm, when I find forgiveness from sin, I still have to deal with a broken bone" (Dallas: Word Publishing, 1997, 210-211).

Grace forgives. Grace brings you into a state of righteousness and holiness before the Lord. Grace restores the presence of God to you. But grace does not cause "crop failure." Grace does not kill the seed that you planted. The pleasure of sin inevitably gives way to the great pain of the harvest. You can count on it every time. And God in His grace allows it to happen so that you will learn not to plant any more bad seeds.

Guidance for Grace: The Word of God

We're not under law but under grace. That means that if and when you sincerely repent and turn to the Lord, He will forgive you. However, it is far better never to plant that bad seed of sin in the first place. God wants us to avoid the painful consequences of sin by choosing to follow His ways. To help us live at peace with Him, with the people around us, and with ourselves while we live on this earth, God has provided principles in His Word to give guidance for our behavior. Although we are no longer under the *burden* of the law to gain right standing with God, we should still consider the basic commands of Scripture as our guidelines for right behavior and right choices as we walk through our lives.

One of the most famous passages of the Bible is Exodus 20:1-17, which outlines for us the Ten Commandments. The Ten Commandments are ten laws, rules, or principles that God gave to Moses to give to the nation of Israel, to teach them how to live happy and free from sin and its misery. God gave these ten laws, not to create legalism or encourage a false behavior-oriented religiosity, but in order to save our lives from destruction, disease, and death.

God is the all-righteous One, and He alone knows all things. He is omniscient; He has all knowledge and wisdom. God knew, for example, that adulterous conduct would destroy the participants. Man did not know this. Only God had this knowledge. So to protect man from destroying himself, God said, "Thou shalt not commit adultery." God is not a tyrant who is trying to spoil our fun and good times. God wants us to have fun, but we must allow Him to define what is fun and what is not. Man thinks that adultery is fun, but God knows better. God knows that it will bring destruction into our lives. This is why God drew a line or made a boundary for us; it is to protect us and prevent us from destroying ourselves. The same is true for the other nine commandments. Each one of the Ten Commandments is a divine boundary line that God has drawn for us to protect us, and to keep us from ruining our lives. The Ten Commandments are ten of the best friends you will ever have! Love them. Learn them. Submit to them. Obey them.

Just as disobedience to the laws of God brings destruction and pain, obedience opens the doors for great blessing, peace, and joy. This is why we need to keep the principles of God and His Word ever before us.

Hear, O Israel: The Lord our God, the Lord is one. Love the Lord your God with all your heart and with all your soul and with all your strength. These commandments that I give you today are to be upon your hearts. Impress them on your children. Talk about them when you sit at home and when you walk along the road, when you lie down and when you get up. Tie them as symbols on your hands and bind them on your foreheads. Write them on the doorframes of your houses and on your gates (Deuteronomy 6:4-9).

We can easily look at the Ten Commandments as ten principles for success. That's right. These ten rules will help you be a success in life. Obeying them will keep you out of troubled areas that can only bring failure to you as a person, to your life, and to the ones you love.

Learn to stay within the divine boundaries that God has drawn. People only destroy themselves and their lives when they step over the lines. Remember, God loves you and is only trying to protect you from destruction and from having an unhappy life. Thank God, He has told us in His Word how to live long, healthy, successful lives.

Although the Ten Commandments are ten absolutes that, along with the other principles of God's Word, teach us right from wrong, they are not the way to be made right with God or to enter Heaven! As we have already seen, the only way to be made righteous is by faith in the atoning death and merits of Jesus Christ.

Let's look at just a few of the Ten Commandments to gain a better understanding of how they help us live better lives.

You shall have no other gods before me (Exodus 20:3).

It is wrong to have any god besides the true and living God whom the Bible describes as the Creator, the God of Abraham, and the God and Father of our Lord Jesus Christ. Any god other than Father God is a false god and must be rejected. It is right to have the true God and wrong to have any other god! This commandment is an absolute! There is no room for compromise on this issue. The gods of all other faiths are unacceptable. Nothing and no one should ever come between us and our relationship with the God of Heaven.

Compare the nation of India to the United States. The United States was built on a belief in the true God and upon the Judeo-Christian heritage. India, on the other hand, is a nation devoted to the false gods of Hinduism, and there are millions of these false gods in the Hindu religion. India suffers with massive plagues, poverty, drought, famine, and rats. It is undoubtedly a cursed land and a religion of false gods and demonism has brought the curse. To get rid of the curse India must turn from the false gods that its people now worship to the Creator God, who is the one and only true and living God. All other gods bring curses and death. The God of the Bible brings blessings and life.

> *Remember the Sabbath day by keeping it holy. Six days you shall labor and do all your work, but the seventh day is a Sabbath to the Lord your God. On it you shall not do any work, neither you, nor your son or daughter, nor your manservant or maidservant, nor your animals, nor the alien within your gates. For in six days the Lord made the heavens and the earth, the sea, and all that is in them, but he rested on the seventh day. Therefore the Lord blessed the Sabbath day and made it holy* (Exodus 20:8-11).

God has asked us to set aside one day to rest and to worship Him. It is wrong to use the Lord's day for yourself. Honoring the Lord Jesus on the Sabbath day or on the Lord's day, which is the New Testament equivalent, is the right thing to do. On the Lord's day we are to gather with believers and worship God together as the Body of Christ. Not only does God deserve our worship, but we need the fellowship and encouragement of other believers and regular teaching from the Word if we are to continue to be successful in our Christian walk. To habitually stay home is wrong (see Heb. 10:25). Christians who are never in church on Sunday are identifying themselves with the lost, unregenerate crowd of the world. With whom do you stand on Sunday—the Church or the crowd who is at home washing their cars and puttering around the house? By taking out a day to worship God we are identifying who we are, we are acknowledging His preeminence in our lives, and we are giving our minds and bodies a much needed rest and change of pace. How many Christians would be in better health physically, emotionally, and spiritually, if they only obeyed this command?

Honor your father and your mother, so that you may live long in the land the Lord your God is giving you (Exodus 20:12).

It is wrong to dishonor your mother and father; God said so. We have chapter and verse to prove it. No exceptions are given to this commandment. God says it is right to honor your parents and wrong to dishonor them. There are no "buts" or exceptions allowed. There is right, and there is wrong, and God has made His will known in this matter. In fact, this commandment is the first commandment with a promise. If we obey this command we are promised to have a long life, full of blessing (see Eph. 6:1-3 NLT).

You shall not commit adultery (Exodus 20:14).

It is wrong to commit adultery. It is right to keep yourself pure and live a sexually pure lifestyle. All adultery is wrong! It is never right to have physically intimate relations with anyone but your spouse. There is no room for compromise here. This commandment protects the sanctity of marriage and the family. Many of our children are suffering today because the amount of sexual promiscuity in the land. These children would not be suffering if we had only stayed within God's divine boundaries. God knows what is good for us and what is not.

You shall not steal (Exodus 20:15).

It is wrong to steal. Stealing means to take something that does not belong to you. It is never right to steal someone else's property. This is an absolute. This commandment protects our possessions and belongings.

As you can see from these examples, the Ten Commandments are for our protection and guidance, and they protect our communities and our relationships with each other and with God. The principles of the Ten Commandments of Exodus 20:1-17 are also incorporated into the pages of the New Testament, not as a means to salvation, but as a by-product of the salvation that comes by faith in Jesus Christ. It comes down to right relationship with God through our Lord Jesus Christ. Relationship and closeness with God is key to the continuing present tense holiness in our lives. In fact, Jesus summed up all the commands of God into the following two commands:

> ..."Love the Lord your God with all your heart and with all your soul and with all your mind." This is the first and greatest commandment. And the second is like it: "Love your neighbor as yourself." All the Law and the Prophets hang on these two commandments (Matthew 22:37-40).

The commandments of God provide us with boundaries that protect our relationships with God and with one another. Even though we are under grace, these boundaries still exist to bless us and protect us. Some religious individuals create sets of rules that are in addition to the divinely inspired commandments of God found in the Bible. When we try to add to the commands, boundaries, and principles that God has already established in His Word, we step over into legalism, which only kills the life of Christ within the believer and many times drives the believer far from God.

Discern God's Ways From Man's

The Bible has already established for us what is right and what is wrong. Your ideas of right and wrong don't really matter. Mine don't either. When the Bible names an activity as sin and we have the chapter and verse to prove it is wrong, then, without a doubt, it is wrong.

We have seen in this book that there are clearly biblical absolutes for our behavior, and God has drawn some boundaries. And there are clear consequences when we violate His holy Word. But what do we do about the things not specifically mentioned in His Word—things like, should a Christian watch television or go to the movies? Should a Christian ever watch an "R" rated movie? Is it right for Christians to go to the beach? Is drinking a glass of wine a sin? If a Christian has a beer is he in sin? Can a Christian play any card games? What if a believer bought a lottery or raffle ticket, is that a sin? Does participation in any of these things make a Christian unholy or worldly? What type of music should a Christian be allowed to listen to? Can a Christian woman wear jewelry or makeup?

When we have God's Word on an issue, it is an absolute expression of the will of God. We have God's Word that states that every believer is already made holy before God because of Christ. We know that we are to walk with the Spirit and follow His guidance to continue to sanctify our minds and our lives. And we are promised that when Christ returns, we shall be made completely perfect. Let's stick with the written Word of God and its absolutes. We have the Word and the Spirit, and we are fully equipped to walk holy and righteously before God. There is no need to add a bunch of man-made rules; neither should we judge a brother or sister who does not choose as we have on an issue that is a disputable matter before the Lord. God gives us rules to help us. Man gives us rules to control us, to take away our freedom in Christ, and make us religious by leaning upon a false understanding of holiness.

In Christ, you have been made holy before God. By the Spirit and the Word, you may now walk righteous and holy before God. God wants you to succeed, and by His grace you have everything you need. Step forth in freedom and walk in true holiness!

Other
Destiny Image titles
you will enjoy reading

NON-RELIGIOUS CHRISTIANITY
by Gerald Coates.
If Jesus Christ returned today, how much of "church" would He condone or condemn? In this book, Gerald Coates contends that "religion" is the greatest hindrance to making Jesus attractive to our family, neighbors, and co-workers. Humorous yet confrontational, this popular British speaker and church leader will surprise you with his conclusions. This book could change your life forever!
ISBN 1-56043-694-8 $9.99p

WHEN GOD STRIKES THE MATCH
by Dr. Harvey R. Brown, Jr.
A noted preacher, college administrator, and father of an "all-American" family—what more could a man want? But when God struck the match that set Harvey Brown ablaze, it ignited a passion for holiness and renewal in his heart that led him into a head-on encounter with the consuming fire of God.
ISBN 0-7684-1000-2 $9.99p

ANOINTED OR ANNOYING?
by Ken Gott.
Don't miss out on the powerful move of God that is in the earth today! When you encounter God's Presence in revival, you have a choice—accept it or reject it; become anointed or annoying! Ken Gott, former pastor of Sunderland Christian Centre and now head of Revival Now! International Ministries, calls you to examine your own heart and motives for pursuing God's anointing, and challenges you to walk a life of obedience!
ISBN 0-7684-1003-7 $9.99p

Available at your local Christian bookstore.

Internet: http://www.reapernet.com

Other
Destiny Image titles
you will enjoy reading

RELEASERS OF LIFE
by Mary Audrey Raycroft.
Inside you is a river that is waiting to be tapped—the river of the Holy Spirit and power! Let Mary Audrey Raycroft, a gifted exhorter and teacher and the Pastor of Equipping Ministries and Women in Ministry at the Toronto Airport Christian Fellowship, teach you how you can release the unique gifts and anointings that the Lord has placed within you. Discover how you can move and minister in God's freeing power and be a releaser of life!
ISBN 1-56043-198-9 $9.99p

THE COSTLY ANOINTING
by Lori Wilke.
In this book, teacher and prophetic songwriter Lori Wilke boldly reveals God's requirements for being entrusted with an awesome power and authority. She speaks directly from God's heart to your heart concerning the most costly anointing. This is a word that will change your life!
ISBN 1-56043-051-6 $9.99p

DON'T DIE IN THE WINTER...
Why do we go through hard times? Why must we suffer pain? In *Don't Die in the Winter...* Dr. Thompson, a pastor, teacher, and conference speaker, explains the spiritual seasons and cycles that people experience. A spiritual winter is simply a season that tests our growth. We need to endure our winters, for in the plan of God, spring always follows winter!
ISBN 1-56043-558-5 $8.99p

Available at your local Christian bookstore.

Internet: http://www.reapernet.com

Other *Destiny Image titles* you will enjoy reading

THE GOD CHASERS
by Tommy Tenney.
Are you dissatisfied with "church"? Are you looking for more? Do you yearn to touch God? You may be a *God chaser*! The passion of Tommy Tenney, evangelist and third-generation Pentecostal minister, is to "catch" God and find himself in God's manifest presence. For too long God's children have been content with crumbs. The Father is looking for those who will seek His face. This book will enflame your own desire to seek God with your whole heart and being—and to find Him.
ISBN 0-7684-2016-4 $10.99p

BEHOLD THE HARVEST
by Dale Rumble.
A final harvest of souls is coming that will be greater than that of all previous revivals! This unique, prophetic study of end-time events reveals how Jesus is going to restore His Church, how children will become warriors in this spiritual army, and many other nuggets of truth!
ISBN 1-56043-192-X $9.99p

ENCOUNTERS WITH A SUPERNATURAL GOD
by Jim and Michal Ann Goll.
The Golls know that angels are real. They have firsthand experience with supernatural angelic encounters. In this book you'll read and learn about angels and supernatural manifestations of God's Presence—and the real encounters that both Jim and Michal Ann have had! As the founders of Ministry to the Nations and speakers and teachers, they share that God wants to be intimate friends with His people. Go on an adventure with the Golls and find out if God has a supernatural encounter for you!
ISBN 1-56043-199-7 $9.99p

Available at your local Christian bookstore.

Internet: http://www.reapernet.com

Prices subject to change without notice.

4:3

Exciting titles
by Don Nori

THE POWER OF BROKENNESS

Accepting Brokenness is a must for becoming a true vessel of the Lord, and is a stepping-stone to revival in our hearts, our homes, and our churches. Brokenness alone brings us to the wonderful revelation of how deep and great our Lord's mercy really is. Join this companion who leads us through the darkest of nights. Discover the *Power of Brokenness*.

ISBN 1-56043-178-4 $9.99p

HIS MANIFEST PRESENCE

This is a passionate look at God's desire for a people with whom He can have intimate fellowship. Not simply a book on worship, it faces our triumphs as well as our sorrows in relation to God's plan for a dwelling place that is splendid in holiness and love.

ISBN 0-914903-48-9 $8.99p
Also available in Spanish.
ISBN 1-56043-079-6 $8.99p

SECRETS OF THE MOST HOLY PLACE

Here is a prophetic parable you will read again and again. The winds of God are blowing, drawing you to His Life within the Veil of the Most Holy Place. There you begin to see as you experience a depth of relationship your heart has yearned for. This book is a living, dynamic experience with God!

ISBN 1-56043-076-1 $9.99p

Available at your local Christian bookstore.

Internet: http://www.reapernet.com

Other
Destiny Image titles
you will enjoy reading

WHEN THE HEAVENS ARE BRASS
by John Kilpatrick.
Pastor John Kilpatrick wanted something more. He began to pray, but it seemed like the heavens were brass. The lessons he learned over the years helped birth a mighty revival in Brownsville Assembly of God that is sweeping through this nation and the world. The dynamic truths in this book could birth life-changing revival in your own life and ministry!
ISBN 1-56043-190-3 $9.99p

A HEART FOR GOD
by Charles P. Schmitt.
This powerful book will send you on a 31-day journey with David from brokenness to wholeness. Few men come to God with as many millstones around their necks as David did. Nevertheless, David pressed beyond adversity, sin, and failure into the very forgiveness and deliverance of God. The life of David will bring hope to those bound by generational curses, those born in sin, and those raised in shame. David's life will inspire faith in the hearts of the dysfunctional, the failure-ridden, and the fallen!
ISBN 1-56043-157-1 $9.99p

THE SHOCK WAVE
by Burton Seavey.
Listen! Do you hear it? The explosion that occurred 2,000 years ago at Pentecost is still reverberating around the world! This next "shock wave" of the Spirit will mature and equip the saints, and sweep vast multitudes into the Kingdom of God—but is the Church ready? Find out how you can prepare in this dynamic book!
ISBN 1-56043-283-7 $13.99p

Available at your local Christian bookstore.
Internet: http://www.reapernet.com

Other
Destiny Image titles
you will enjoy reading

THE THREE PREJUDICES
by Kelley Varner.
Three walls of prejudice are still blocking God's power from flowing as freely and as strongly as He desires. Our fear of rejection and our misconceptions build these walls between us and our fellow believers. Learn the truth from the Bible about gender, race, and nations!
ISBN 1-56043-187-3 $9.99p

PERCEIVING THE WHEEL OF GOD
by Dr. Mark Hanby.
On the potter's wheel, a lump of clay yields to a necessary process of careful pressure and constant twisting. Similarly, the form of true faith is shaped by a trusting response to the hand of God in a suffering situation. This book offers essential understanding for victory through the struggles of life.
ISBN 1-56043-109-1 $9.99p

IT'S TIME TO ROCK THE BOAT
by Dr. Michael L. Brown.
Here is a book whose time has come. It is a radical, noncompromising, no-excuse call to genuine Christian activism: intercessory prayer and the action that one must take as a result of that prayer.
ISBN 1-56043-106-7 $9.99p

Available at your local Christian bookstore.

Internet: http://www.reapernet.com